Paddington Station
1833–1854

A Study of the Procurement of Land for,
and Construction of, the First London Terminus
of the Great Western Railway

Michael Tutton

RAILWAY & CANAL HISTORICAL SOCIETY

This book is dedicated
to the memory of my grandfather,
Harold Bygrave, railwayman.

First published in 1999
by the Railway & Canal Historical Society
Registered office: Fron Fawnog, Hafod Road, Gwernymynydd, Mold, Clwyd CH7 5JS
Registered charity no.256047

ISBN 0 901461 20 2

Designed and typeset by Malcolm Preskett
Printed in England by Biddles Ltd, Guildford, Surrey

Cover illustrations
front: looking across the goods yard of the first station at Paddington
with the tower of St Mary's in the distance, 1838 (see FIG.19)
back: an engraving from the *Illustrated London News* of 1843,
looking across the entrance of the station towards what is now
Eastbourne Terrace (based on the sketch shown as FIG.18)

Contents

Preface

THIS study is based on a dissertation for the post-graduate diploma in Industrial Archaeology at The Ironbridge Institute (formerly The Institute of Industrial Archaeology), and Birmingham University which I completed in 1986. Chapters one to five, those dealing with the procurement of land, the site and construction, draw largely on the archives of the Great Western Railway, which comprise part of British Transport Historical Records, held at the Public Record Office, Kew. Chapter six is a glimpse, and only a glimpse, of Paddington at work in its very early years, and draws heavily on MacDermot and Clinker (note 1).

The money figures quoted throughout the text and appendices are at contemporary values and need to be multiplied by a factor of 56 to bring them to current (1999) values.

Special mention needs to be made of the early plans of Paddington Station, FIGS 13 to 16. FIG.13 was reproduced in MacDermot in redrawn form, and again in the Railway Gazette Supplement of August 1935 (FIG.11). The other plans, as far as I know, have never been published before. I had access to this material in the mid-1980s at British Rail (Western), Swindon and I was given prints from microfiche for my dissertation, and the option, which unfortunately I did not take up, of having photographic prints made from the originals. Railtrack granted permission to photograph them, but then could not find the originals, which are therefore either lost, destroyed or otherwise disposed of. The illustrations are therefore reproduced from the microfiche prints and this explains their less than perfect reproduction. Acknowledgement must therefore go to: the late British Rail (Western), Railtrack Great Western and the Ironbridge Gorge Museum Trust Library.

Other sources are referred to and acknowledged in the notes and captions.

I am grateful to the following: Alan A. Jackson and Graham Boyes for reading the text and bringing several points to my notice and making various corrections, staff at the Public Record Office and Westminster Archives Centre, and Malcolm Preskett for his constant help during the production phase of this book and his excellent design and layout.

Michael Tutton
APRIL 1999

ONE

Introduction

THE Great Western Railway dates back to the autumn of 1832. Following on the success of the Stockton & Darlington and Liverpool & Manchester Railways and in a climate of increasing railway promotion, a scheme was formulated to link Bristol with London.[1] In its early years the scheme was essentially a Bristol affair and despite a London committee and twelve London directors the precise location of a London terminus was somewhat vague and uncertain – a situation which lasted some four years.

Despite this, however, the Great Western Railway avoided the controversy which attended the choice of site and construction of many other termini in the Capital.[2] There were several reasons for this:

— the sites eventually selected for the terminus and its approaches were on open ground;

— very little demolition was required and only some slight alteration to the line of the Harrow Road was necessary;

— Paddington was not at that time within the Metropolis.

The Company did experience problems conveying their passengers to and from the City, which led them later to support and invest in the first underground railway, from Paddington to Farringdon Road in the City.[3]

In common with most other railway companies building lines to the capital, the Great Western Railway stopped short of central London. However, apart from their involvement in the Metropolitan Railway they did not find it necessary to penetrate further into London, as did other companies, with often crippling financial consequences, not to mention the upheaval, and displacement suffered by the occupiers of the land through which these extensions passed.[4]

The Great Western Railway did need to rebuild its London terminus in the early 1850s; however this must be seen as a planned expansion rather than the pressing and sometimes desperate need to enlarge or extend inadequate and inefficient facilities.

When the Company finally decided on a site for the terminus they took the decision, in the light of the uncertain nature of passenger traffic in the 1830s, to erect only temporary buildings and depots on the site until such time as the traffic warranted more permanent facilities. It is the history of this temporary terminus that this study will attempt to explore.

1. See E.T. MacDermot, *History of the Great Western Railway,* Great Western Railway Co., London 1927, Vol.1: 1833–1863 (the standard work on the Great Western Railway). Revised edition by C.R. Clinker published 1964.

2. See J.R. Kellett, *Railways and Victorian Cities,* 1969, chapter IX and *passim.*

3. See T.C. Barker & M. Robbins, *History of London Transport,* 1963, Vol.1, chapter 4.

4. Kellett, op.cit., and H.J. Dyos, 'Railways and Housing in Victorian London' and 'Some Social Costs of Railway Building in London', in *Exploring the Urban Past – Essays in Urban History,* 1982.

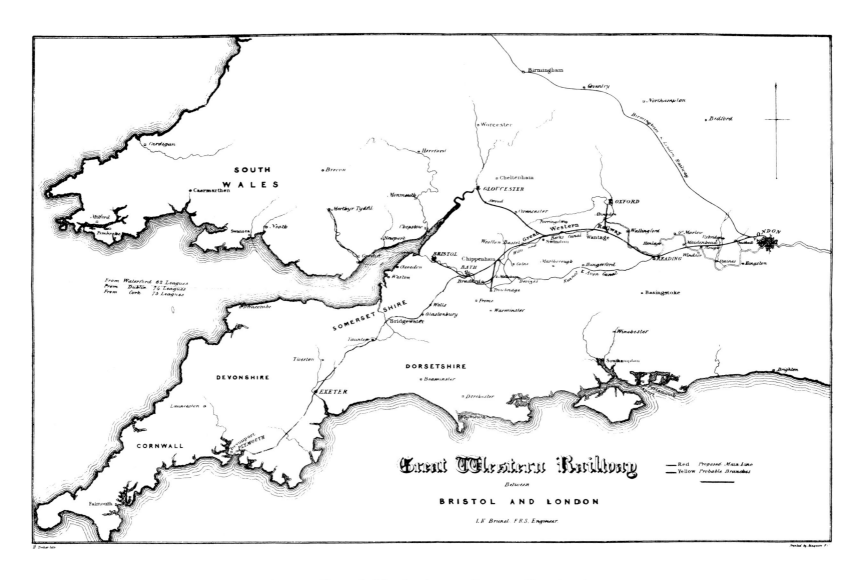

1. Prospectus Plan, 2nd edition, Supplementary Prospectus, November 1834.
The Great Western Railway as planned in November 1834 showing the junction with the London and Birmingham Railway and several branches.
(Public Record Office)

TWO

Early Schemes

THE report, dated 30 July 1833, of the committee of deputies appointed by the City of Bristol and comprising the Civic Corporation, the Society of Merchant Venturers, the Bristol Dock Company, the Bristol Chamber of Commerce and the Bristol & Gloucester Railway Company, states:

> The total length of the Railway would be from 115 to 118, or 120 miles, depending on its termination, whether at Paddington, or some part of the Southern bank of the Thames.[5]

At the first meeting of the Board of Directors in London on 30 August 1833 the minutes record the following:

> Having reference at the same time to the Prospectus and Plan prepared in conformity with former resolutions, it was considered expedient to make an alteration in them so as to show two lines of Road from Maidenhead to London, also to explain that no course has yet been finally adopted.[6]

The resolutions alluded to would have been taken at the first

joint meeting of the Bristol and London Committees, also held in London, on 19 August, some ten days earlier, and at which, according to MacDermot, the first prospectus was settled and, incidentally, the title Great Western Railway adopted.[7]

The plan accompanying the prospectus dated August 1833, shows one line terminating at what is presumably Paddington. The second line crosses the Thames below Kingston and terminates south of the river approximately between Westminster and Waterloo bridges (FIG.2). This second line was fairly soon abandoned as it does not appear in any subsequent prospectus or minute.

The first definite site for a London terminus dates to October 1833. A second prospectus in the form of a circular states the Company's intention to apply to Parliament in the coming session for authority to construct the line at its extremities only, i.e. from Bristol to Bath and from Reading to London. This was because insufficient capital had been subscribed. It was a Parliamentary Standing Order that at least half of the capital should be subscribed before a Bill could proceed, and the directors did not want to wait until the next session.

The plan now shows only one route into London (FIG.3). In a letter to Philip Hardwick, the London surveyor, Charles Saunders, the London Secretary, expresses, at least in part, the feelings of the London Committee:

> . . . I need scarcely point out to you how pressing it is upon the Committee to make some progress with the negotiations near London, before the plans can be finally

2. Prospectus Plan, 2nd issue of First Prospectus, 1 August 1833. Detail: Reading to London showing the alternative route and terminus south of the river. (Public Record Office)

5. 'BRISTOL AND LONDON RAILWAY. At a numerous and respectable meeting of INHABITANTS of BRISTOL and its neighbourhood, desirous of assisting in the Establishment of a RAILWAY to LONDON held (pursuant to public advertisement) at the GUILDHALL, BRISTOL, on Tuesday, the 30th day of July, 1833' – 'REPORT of the Provisional Committee . . .' etc. Copy in Science Museum, London.

6. Public Record Office (PRO), RAIL 250/1, Board Minutes, 30/8/1833.

7. Quoted in MacDermot, op.cit., p.4.

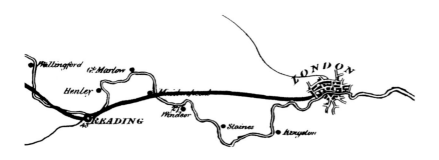

passed into the committee stage which took some 57 days starting on 16 April 1834.

The Company's principal engineering witness was Isambard Kingdom Brunel who had been appointed engineer in March 1833. He was asked at an early stage, 2 May 1834, whether the promoters would press for a terminus at Vauxhall or terminate the line some two miles further west at Brompton on a site to the rear of the 'Hoop and Toy' public house in the Old Brompton Road. The latter course was adopted at a meeting of the Board of Directors on 3 May 1834.

There had been much negotiation and wrangling with landowners between Brompton and Vauxhall, some of whom were influential members of the House of Lords; principal among them was Lord Cadogan who opposed the Bill.[10]

The Bill passed the House of Commons and proceeded to the Lords where it was rejected on the second reading on 25 July by 47 to 30, in part due, no doubt, to Cadogan's opposition, but largely due to that House's opposition to a line

3 (above). Prospectus Plan, 3rd issue of First Prospectus, 13 March 1834. Detail: Reading to London showing the route to Vauxhall Bridge. (Public Record Office)

4 (right). Parliamentary Deposited Plan, November 1833. Detail: Hanwell to London. These plans were highly-detailed 'ribbon' maps showing individual plots of land through which the line passed and adjacent features and buildings. Books of Reference gave details of landowners and tenants etc. (see appendix A). (Public Record Office)

drawn, or the preliminary enquiries as to names of Owners and Occupants be undertaken.[8]

The plans deposited at the end of November show a line from South Acton through Hammersmith, Brompton, Pimlico to a terminus at Vauxhall Bridge [9] (FIGS 3, 4 & 6). The second Commons reading of the Bill for this line was moved on 10 March 1834 and carried by 182 votes to 92; it then

8. PRO RAIL 253/85, General Letter Book, London Committee, 5/10/1833.

9. PRO RAIL 252/2, Parliamentary Deposited Plan, November 1833.

10. PRO RAIL 250/1, Board Minutes, 11/3/1834, and Rail 253/85, General Letter Book, London Committee, Saunders to Lord Cadogan 1/5/1834 and Saunders to Wm Lee (Solicitor for the opposing counsel) 5/5/1834.

11. PRO RAIL 250/1, Board Minutes, 2/9/1834.

12. MacDermot, op.cit., 1927, pp.8–9.

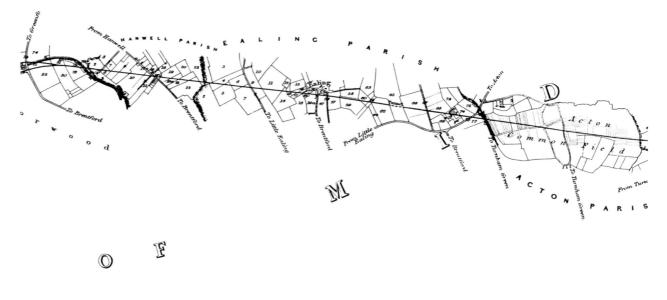

which on the face of it was two short lines with a vast gap between them.

The Company immediately began preparations for bringing a Bill for the whole line before Parliament in the next year. A supplementary prospectus was issued in September 1834, which although hinting at a change of direction near London left the site of the London terminus unspecified. The landowners of Kensington, Chelsea and Pimlico were ever more immovable and Brompton was dropped. This prospectus, inviting subscriptions for the additional shares required for the whole line, was authorised at a meeting of the Board of Directors on 2 September 1834, at which it was also:

> Resolved that it is expedient to authorise a negotiation with the London and Birmingham Company for the purpose of ascertaining and determining whether a junction might be made with their line at or near Harlesden Green, and that the London Committee be empowered to undertake that duty.[11]

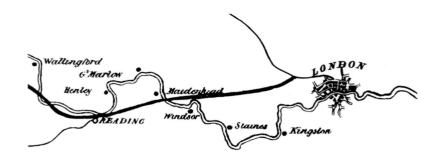

A second edition of the supplementary prospectus was issued in November which states:

> The line of railway is described in the annexed plan. It will be 114 miles in length from Bristol to the point of junction with the Birmingham Line near Wormwood Scrubs. The station for Passengers is intended to be near the New Road in the Parish of St Pancras.[12]
> (FIGS 1 & 5)

5. Prospectus Plan, 2nd edition, Supplementary Prospectus, November 1834.
Detail: Reading to London showing the junction with the London and Birmingham Railway. (Public Record Office)

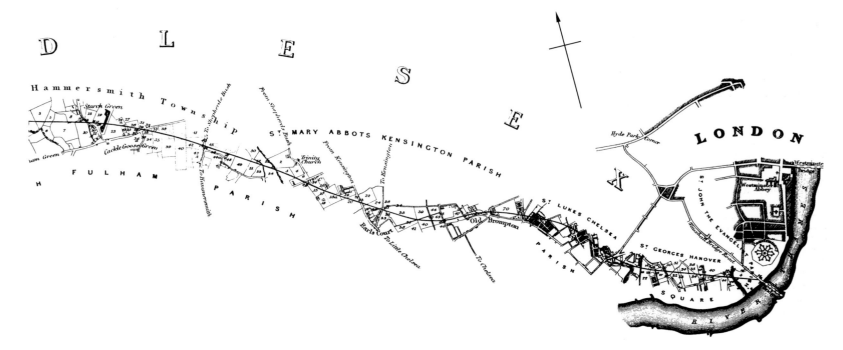

So Euston became the next site for a London terminus, shared with the London & Birmingham Railway, a scheme fraught with difficulties.

The earliest reference to a joint terminus is a letter from Saunders to Richard Creed, his counterpart at the London & Birmingham, dated 12 August 1834, referring to an extract of Minutes with reference to a junction, but giving no further details.[13] This was followed by another letter on 3 September, which followed the resolution adopted on the 2nd, and referred to evidence given by Robert Stephenson, engineer to the London & Birmingham Railway:

> . . . before the committee of the House of Commons
> as to the practicability of uniting the Bristol Railway
> with that of the London and Birmingham near
> Harlesden Green to the mutual advantage of the two
> Companies . . .[14]

Exactly who, originally, proposed such a junction is not clear but the idea clearly dates back to the period May/June 1834 when Brompton as a terminus site was still under consideration.

The negotiations for a junction with the London & Birmingham Railway occupied almost 18 months, a period which represented a considerable waste of time, effort and money. This period also saw the passing of a Bill for the whole line which included such a junction, the Great Western Railway Act of 31 August 1835, the floundering of an agreement which had barely been reached let alone substantiated or ratified despite the passing of the Act[15], and the adoption of a resolution to seek yet another site and, by implication, another Bill to authorise it.

The long drawn-out negotiations were over-shadowed by the question of gauge. Brunel first mentioned the wide gauge in his report to the Board of Directors dated 15 September 1835, only 15 days after the passing of the Act on 31 August, and the resolution formally adopting it was taken at a Board meeting on 29 October 1835. It is not known exactly when Brunel decided to recommend the broad gauge; he said himself:

I think the impression grew upon me gradually, so that it is difficult to fix the time when I first thought a wide gauge desirable; but I daresay there were stages between wishing that it could be so and determining to try and do it.[16]

What is fundamental here is that Brunel knew Robert Stephenson well – they were professional rivals, not least on the question of gauge, but enjoyed firm friendship. Brunel must have known, therefore, that Stephenson, never mind the London & Birmingham's directors, would never accede to the broad gauge at Euston, mixed or otherwise, and if Brunel ever seriously entertained the idea, he surely had his head in the clouds. This is borne out by the minutes of the board meeting of 29 October 1835:

> Mr Brunel reported that he had had an interview with
> Mr Robt. Stephenson the Engineer of the London and
> Birmingham Railway Company who expressed his
> impression that he would advise the Directors of the
> London and Birmingham Railway Company not to
> accede to the proposals to lay rails of a greater span
> on that Railway.[17]

There follows the above-mentioned resolution adopting the 7-foot gauge.

Much of the negotiations were taken up in determining the amount of land required by the Great Western Railway and whether it would be purchased or taken on some kind of lease, proposals for running the joint station and line, and whether there would be equal advantages and accommodation. They are fairly well summed up in the Report of the Directors to the first half-yearly meeting of Shareholders held on 26 February 1836, the relevant part of which is worth quoting in full:

> . . . The Directors consider it a duty upon this
> occasion to apprise the Proprietors [that] the
> proposals recently made to them by the London and
> Birmingham Railway Company with regard to the
> contemplated junction of the two lines, are not such
> as they would have been justified in accepting.

13. PRO RAIL 253/85, General Letter Book, London Committee, 12/8/1834.

14. Ibid., 3/9/1834.

15. Although the London and Birmingham initially laid out Euston to allow for the Great Western Railway terminus alongside theirs. (I am indebted to Mr Alan A. Jackson for bringing this to my notice.)

16. Quoted in L.T.C. Rolt, *Isambard Kingdom Brunel*, Longmans 1957, p.108.

17. PRO RAIL 250/2, Board Minutes, 29/10/1835.

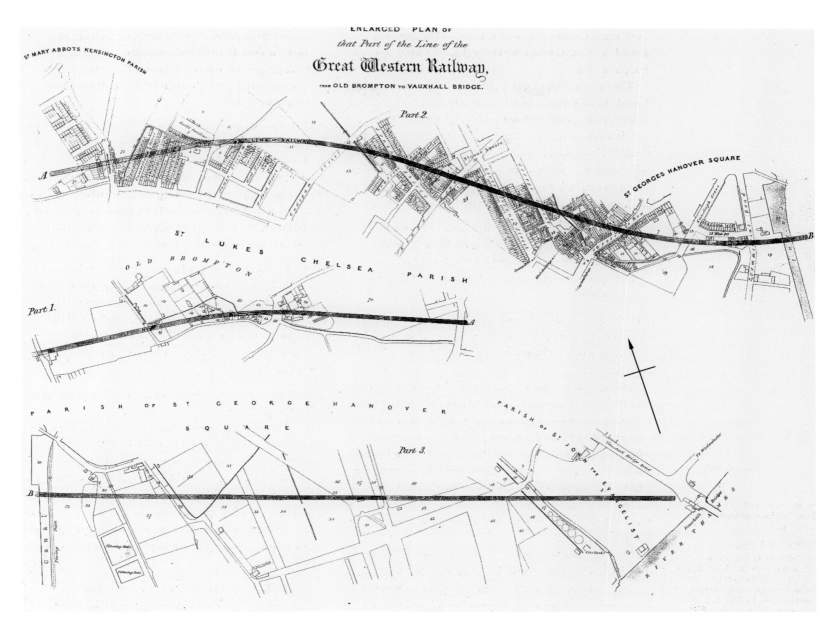

6. Parliamentary Deposited Plan, November 1833, enlarged part, Kensington to Vauxhall Bridge.
(Public Record Office)

In November last, after protracted negotiations with the London Committee of that Company a deputation from the Great Western Railway attended a meeting of the General Board of Directors at Birmingham for the purpose of finally concerting and deciding the general conditions of the junction. The pecuniary terms occasioned a very protracted discussion and were settled. The claim for an allotment of sufficient land for the purposes of depots and station houses both at Camden Town and Euston Grove, referred to in previous conferences with the London Committee, was recognised and admitted.

This question, being one of vital importance to the interests of the public and of the Proprietors, invariably formed a prominent part in the proposals made by your Directors, who had always represented that the acquisition of land by purchase or at least upon a Building Lease was indispensable as the only guarantee for an arrangement of such permanency as could justify them in incurring the unavoidable expense of the junction. It is a matter of regret that the refusal of the London and Birmingham Directors to grant the allotment of land upon such terms should have been delayed until the month of December when for the first time objections were raised to that condition.

With a sincere desire, however, to accomplish the Junction by concession, your Directors, after relinquishing their claim first to a purchase of the land, and next to a building lease, finally substituted a proposal to take a lease of 21 years only, as the shortest term for which it would be consistent with their duty to accept the allotment, to which it is acknowledged they were entitled.

They felt the propriety, and even the necessity of this course, the more, from its having come to their knowledge that a large and influential body of distant Proprietors were urging the directors of the London and Birmingham Railway to retain in their hands the power of breaking off any arrangements that might be made with the Great Western Railway Company at the shortest possible notice as well from a hope of afterwards obtaining higher pecuniary terms, as from a fear that there would not be room for the traffic of both the lines, and their respective branches at the depots.

Under these circumstances, the directors of the London and Birmingham Railway, not acquiescing in the lease of 21 years, offered at a recent meeting, to grant a portion of the land at the depot, subject to be resumed by them upon a notice of 5 years, which your directors have had no hesitation in declining, under the conviction that the permanency of the junction would be thereby defeated, entertaining also a confident belief that an excellent and independent terminus can be secured without difficulty at latest in the next session of Parliament.[18]

Almost exactly a year before the deputation from the Great Western Railway attended the board meeting of the London & Birmingham in November 1835, there appeared in the London Committee Minutes for 30 October 1834 the following:

After a conference with Mr Brunel as to the course to be pursued in amending the Parliamentary notices by the addition of a line to Paddington, or elsewhere, to be adopted as an alternative in case the agreement already made for the junction with that Company should be negatived by their Board of Directors.

And on 5 November 1834:

Resolved. That the determination of the London Committee of the Birmingham Company to adhere to the agreement with this Company . . . induces this Committee to rely entirely on the Agreement already made for the junction with the Birmingham Railway in which case it becomes inexpedient to amend the Parliamentary notices so as to include a branch to Paddington.[19]

18. PRO RAIL 250/64, General Meetings of Proprietors, Oct.1835 to Aug.1844, 26/2/1836.

19. PRO RAIL 250/84, Minutes, London Committee 30/10/1834 and 5/11/1834.

Brunel seems never to have been whole-heartedly in favour of the junction and joint terminus. This can be read 'between the lines' in his reports to the Board. In his report of 14 September 1835 he alludes to possible difficulties and impracticalities and urges that arrangements be immediately made so that if any such difficulties do appear, the necessary Parliamentary notices can be given before 1 November for a separate entrance into London. His main concern here was to have the first part of the line, between Maidenhead and London, open by his promised date of October 1837.

His next report, on the very next day, is that which contains his suggestion as to gauge. He gave four possible objections to a 7-foot gauge, the first three being unimportant here, but the fourth is the difficulty and inconvenience of the junction – which he considered the only real obstacle saying that the additional rail to be laid down, i.e. mixed gauge, was not a (technical) problem, but – and this is the crux of the matter – the London & Birmingham may object to it.[20]

Again in his report dated 8 October 1835[21] he urged decision on any matters which required application to Parliament in the ensuing session, again mentioning a separate entrance into London. In his report of 19 November[22] he referred to Robert Stephenson's willingness to consider the junction, but alluded to the fact that any successor to him or new directors might have different views, thus placing the Great Western Railway under enormous disadvantage. Another penetrating point raised in this report is the difference between the two companies' perception of what a major terminus should be, and the 'degree of accommodation and inducements' offered to the public, and the London & Birmingham's limited idea of such facilities. The fact that Paddington, once the permanent buildings were erected, has remained largely unaltered and that the 'hotchpotch' that was Euston had to be rationalised and rebuilt in the 1960s bears witness to this. The report also gives us a picture of what the joint terminus and line would have been like.

The question of whether the Great Western Railway should actually purchase land at Euston or be tenants was at this stage not decided, but Brunel and Stephenson assumed that the arrangement would be on the basis of a tenancy. The land purchased at Euston by the London & Birmingham would be divided longitudinally into two parts, the western half being devoted to the Great Western and the eastern to the London & Birmingham, the space between being common to both. The station building fronting Euston Square would be designed by an architect appointed jointly by both companies.

To prevent any competition as to the times of departing trains, a train from each company would start and ascend the inclined plane (the method by which the line from Euston to Camden Town was to operate) together, separated by a train length. Quite how this would be accomplished is not made clear. The London & Birmingham would construct and maintain all permanent way and supply all power, machinery and ropes for the inclined plane.

At Camden Town a sufficient area of land with frontage to the Regent's Canal would be provided for a goods depot and warehouse, as well as engine sheds and repair shops, exclusively for the Great Western. Yards for cattle and market produce, and sidings for carriages would be common and subject to mutual arrangements.

The potential in all this for disruption on a grand scale defies imagination.

Throughout the eighteen months from June 1834 to the end of 1835 the directors seem to have been content to let discussions with the London & Birmingham take their course, despite their protracted nature and the problems involved. There is very little evidence to suggest that Brunel addressed the problem before the latter months of 1835. This is a curious situation, for when the Great Western Railway finally applied to Parliament for an Act to extend the line into Paddington, the scheme, although certain calculated risks were taken, was comparatively problem free, and there is no reason to suggest that this would not have been otherwise in July 1833 when Paddington is first mentioned. It would seem that the only reason for the Company going down the 'blind alley' to Euston was simply bad planning.[23]

20. PRO RAIL 250/82, I.K. Brunel's Reports to the Board of Directors, 14 & 15/9/1835.

21. Ibid., 8/10/1835.

22. Ibid., 19/11/1835.

23. Board minutes of the London & Birmingham Railway covering the period September 1834 through February 1836 (RAIL 384/2) were consulted but nothing of significance concerning the junction came to light.

THREE

Paddington

7 (right). Topographical Survey of the Borough of St Marylebone. Bartlett and Britton, 1834. The area indicated by the figure '3' represents the estates of the Bishop of London with the intended street pattern laid out. Bishop's Walk broadly corresponds with the present Bishop's Bridge and Bishop's Bridge Road. Praed Street, the continuation of which (then named Conduit Street) forms the southern extremity of the site, can be seen between the north and south reservoirs. (City of Westminster Archives Centre)

24. PRO RAIL 250/64, General Meetings of Proprietors Oct.1835 to Aug.1844, 25/8/1836.

25. J. Simmons, *The Birth of the Great Western Railway – Extracts from the Diary and Correspondence of George Henry Gibbs*, Adams & Dart, Bath 1971, p.19.

26. Ibid., p.21.

27. Ibid., and entry for 13 May 1836, pp.21–22.

28. Ibid., entry for 7 June 1836, pp.22–23.

As already mentioned the idea of a terminus at Paddington was toyed with from the very beginning. Throughout the negotiations with the London and Birmingham there appeared from time to time, in the minutes of the London Committee and Board Meetings, mention of provision for an alternative line and terminus, should the negotiations not succeed. This alternative, although not always named as such, must be Paddington.

On 20 February 1836 the Company received a letter from Richard Creed making a final offer of land at Euston on a five year lease – a decision taken at a Board meeting of the London & Birmingham Railway on 17 February. This, as we have seen, was declined – a decision taken by the Great Western Board on 25 February – and the problem of an alternative site now had to be tackled once and for all. However, they had already attempted, in the current session of Parliament, to present a Bill for the line to Paddington but permission to proceed with this had been refused by the Select Committee on Standing Orders, to whom the Bill had been referred. Whether this was on a technicality or because the Bill was too hastily put together is not clear – from 1836, Standing Orders began to lay down more stringent rules with regard to railway Bills. Whatever the reason it represented a costly waste of time, for the application was made at the very beginning of the Session, February 1836, and they had to wait another year before being able to apply again.

In the Report of the Directors to the second half-yearly meeting held on 25 August 1836[24] reference is made to a cessation of negotiations with the London & Birmingham coming at a time of inconvenience in relation to Parliamentary proceedings, but this is inconvenience of their own

making. George Gibbs, a director, records in his diary for 12 March 1836:

> The section for our new terminus proceeds slowly, and I do not expect that we shall be able to get that line this year.[25]

In other words no application could be made to Parliament in the current session. Again on 23 April he recorded that the question of the terminus lingers on:

> . . . and, notwithstanding the Paddington meeting, [held earlier in the day] I am afraid we shall not do anything this year . . . . The difficulties attending the arrangements with the landowners have driven us to so advanced a period of the Session that there is little hope of obtaining our terminus.[26]

The Session, in fact, was barely halfway through. It opened on 14 February and closed on 20 August 1836. In the next entry, for 8 May, Gibbs recorded more favourable progress with the landowners; and also Saunders' suggestion that a clause – covering the 4.5 mile extension from Acton – be added to the Bill already before Parliament. The clause was duly added, however, having set up a sub-committee to consider the matter, the Company decided to withdraw the clause, mainly for procedural reasons. The Bill in question concerned several small alterations in the line elsewhere. Known as the Deviation Bill, it was passed un-opposed later in the year.[27]

The Company then took the extraordinary step of going ahead with the extension without an Act. They were confident that they had the consent of all the owners,

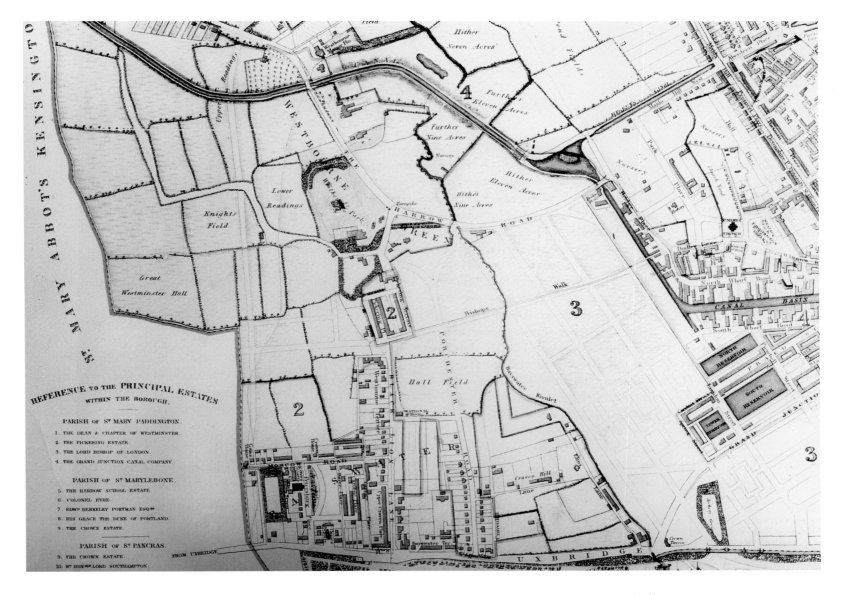

occupiers and parishes from whom they were obtaining the land. Furthermore, they considered the risk of not obtaining the Act and the expense thereby incurred in compensation and returning the land to its former condition – estimated by Gibbs to be between £25,000 and £50,000 – worth taking.[28]

An expensive mistake had things gone wrong, but it paid off and the Act was finally passed on 3 July 1837. Works at Paddington had to wait for the Act, involving as they did an alteration in the line of the Harrow Road – something which could not be attempted without the sanction of Parliament.

FOUR

The Site

29. Blomfield was Bishop from 1828 to 1856; his predecessor, William Howley, from 1813 to 1828. See: B. Denny, *King's Bishop – The Lords Spiritual of London*, 1985; and for the Paddington Estate: W. Robins, *Paddington Past and Present*, 1853. Privately printed by the author. Copy in City of Westminster Archives Centre.

30. Simmons, op.cit., p.20.

31. John Cockerell was the son of Samuel Pepys Cockerell. Westbourne Place was the home of Rowland 1st Viscount Hill (1771–1842), Wellington's second-in-command, eventually succeeding him. He is commemorated by Lord Hill's Bridge, the fourth out of Paddington. The house, which was also for a time occupied by Charles Saunders as his official residence, stood slightly north of the site of the present Porchester Road Library and was demolished by the GWR in 1846.

32. Parish of Paddington, Vestry Minutes, City of Westminster Archives Centre.

33. The term originates with a charity dating back to c.1665 when bread and cheese was thrown to the poor from the steeple of Paddington Church (St James, not the present St Mary's). The custom was established by two women who purchased five acres of land in the parish: F.N. McDonald, *A Short History of Paddington*, 1876, pp.81–3. Copy in City of Westminster Archives Centre.

34. Paddington Vestry Minutes, op. cit., 19/4/1836.

35. Ibid., 26/4/1836.

36. Ibid.

37. Ibid., 19/1/1837 & 26/1/1837.

38. Ibid., 4/2/1837.

39. Bishop's Bridge Road and Bishop's Bridge. Spring Street is now Eastbourne Terrace.

THE SITE selected for the terminus was on open land, bounded to the east by the Paddington branch of the Grand Junction Canal (FIG.7). The land belonged to the Paddington estate of the Bishop of London and had been in possession of the See since the 16th century. In the years leading up to the incorporation of the Great Western Railway, the then Bishop, Charles James Blomfield, and his predecessor[29] had embarked upon ambitious building schemes on the estate especially in the Bayswater area.

These were to the plans of Samuel Pepys Cockerell, surveyor to the estate, and his successor (from 1827), George Gutch. Gutch's plan of 1828 (FIG.8) shows these developments between Conduit Street (now Praed Street) and the Bayswater Road. The area north of Conduit Street – although laid out on the plan – was then open country and park land. The fact that these developments were planned, with continuations of Ranelagh, Westbourne and Spring Streets, probably accounts for the 'enormously high price' the Bishop and the Trustees of the Paddington Estate asked for the 44 acres or so that the Great Western Railway required for their terminus.[30]

Other landowners from whom the company purchased land were: the Grand Junction Canal Co., who had previously purchased the land from the Paddington Estate; a small lot from the Vestry of Paddington; John Cockerell, owner of Westbourne Place;[31] and a few small plots from John Scales (see APPENDIX A).

There are very few records of negotiations between the Company and the Bishop of London and the Trustees of the Paddington Estate. However, those for the purchase of the small piece of land from the Parish of Paddington are fairly well documented.[32]

In April 1836 the Company approached the Vestry of Paddington with a view to purchasing a small plot of land known as the Bread and Cheese Lands.[33] This application was made at a special meeting of the Vestry on 19 April at which Saunders and another officer of the Company submitted a plan of the proposed terminus. The minutes of this meeting record that the terminus was to be near the Wooden Bridge, presumably the bridge which carries the Bishop's Walk – a footpath from Pickering Terrace to Bridge Place – across the canal.[34] (FIG.7)

The application was referred to a committee, which included George Gutch, who reported back to the Vestry on 26 April expressing the opinion that the terminus would be highly beneficial to the Parish.[35] The report goes on to stipulate various conditions which involve making a new carriage road 60 feet wide, broadly following the line of Bishop's Walk, from Black Lion Lane (now Queensway) to the canal at the site of the wooden bridge and replacing that by a 40-foot wide carriage bridge. The level of the railway was to be below that of this new road, thus making it a bridge or viaduct, which became known as Bishop's Bridge. There was a clause for the repair of the parish roads during construction works. It was recommended that the title of the parochial authorities be accepted without requiring the production of any title deeds, 'the estate having been in possession of the parish considerably above one hundred years.'[36] In return for these conditions the Vestry would submit a petition to Parliament in support of the proposed Bill.

The Company agreed to the conditions and a purchase price of £1,200 for the freehold was asked for by the Vestry. Having reached an agreement, however, the Vestry embarked upon what seems to be a campaign of adding new conditions at every available opportunity. At a meeting of the Vestry on 19 January 1837 a third report of the committee was read which repeated the contents of the first two, but added various conditions concerning sewers, road levels and the intended bridge at the intersection of Black Lion Lane (Lord Hill's Bridge) be no less that 40 feet wide. Again at a meeting on 26 January there was a further resolution regarding the approaches to Lord Hill's Bridge and a condition stating that certain of the new roads and bridges be completed within 12 months of the passing of the Act.[37] All of this resulted in a somewhat vitriolic letter from Saunders complaining of the delays and new conditions and inferring that unless the agreement was finalised the Company would cease negotiation, wait for the Act and take the land under powers granted by the Act – in other words compulsory purchase. He then concluded the letter by conceding most of the conditions.[38]

The basis of the final agreement was formulated at a meeting of the Vestry on 4 February 1837, which was attended by Saunders and Brunel, the main points being:

1st   That a Road including footpaths of the width of 60 feet from Black Lion Lane to Spring Street and from thence to the Harrow Road (45 feet) should be made by the company.[39]

2nd   Carriage Bridge in lieu of Wooden Bridge (40 ft).

3rd   Level of the Rail road to be sunk below the present level of the carriage Road where it cross same.

4th   Compensation clause for the extra expense occasioned in the repairs of the parish roads during the progress of the works.

5th   Company to take Bread and Cheese land at £1,200 and accept title.

8. Plan of the Parish of Paddington. George Gutch, 1828.
This plan shows the intended development of the Paddington estates of the Bishop of London as laid out by Samuel Pepys Cockerell and George Gutch.
(Guildhall Library, Corporation of London)

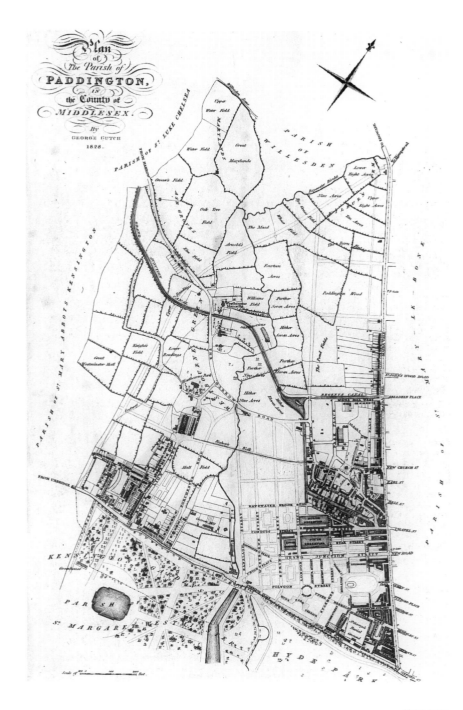

6th To form all sewers necessary to carry off any flow of water arising from any alteration in the level of the line of road.

7th Carriage Road to be made according to 62nd clause of Act.[40]

8th Bridge over the Railway at the intersection of Black Lion Lane[41] shall not be of less than 40-feet wide with modification as to the end according to Mr Saunders' letter of the . . . [42]

9th Clerk's fees to be paid by the company not exceeding £31.10.00.

10th The centre of the Road from the Canal to the Harrow Road to be made in a line with the wooden bridge.

11th To make the Road from the Harrow Road and the Bridge over the canal to the Royal Oak in Black Lion Lane within 18 months after the Act.

12th Clause for the immediate payment of purchase or its deposit in the treasurer's hands in the name of George Carr Glyn on the part of the Company and of Mr William Harris, Churchwarden, on the part of the Parish.[43]

This agreement was confirmed on 9 February and on 13 February the Vestry signed and forwarded their petition to the House of Commons in support of the Bill.

In the meantime negotiations with the Bishop of London and the Trustees of the Paddington Estate were going ahead and agreement was reached a little time after that with the Vestry, being confirmed on 16 February.[44] However, as already mentioned, records of these negotiations are scant, but what survives points to problems, and the following letter dated 11 July from Saunders to Budd & Hayes, Solicitors for the Trustees of the Paddington Estate, exemplifies this:

> I have been desired by the Directors of this Co. to acquaint you that they are about to make their final arrangements with a view to procuring an extension of their line into the immediate neighbourhood of London for which purpose application will be made in the ensuing session of Parliament.

It is unnecessary to (revert) to the nature of the unexpected obstacles which they encountered in the arrangements with the trustees of the Paddington Estate at the moment when they were preparing to make application for the Bill in the present session with the consent of every owner on the line then projected to Paddington.

The Directors, although compelled by the conditions then proposed to suspend their proceedings, are willing to believe that it can be consistent with the interest of the Trustees of the Paddington Estate to allow the disposal of a considerable portion of that property for the purposes required or to oblige the Great Western Railway Co. to seek a Terminus for the line in another direction. Under this impression therefore they can avail themselves of an alternative which has been offered. I am desired to state that the Directors are willing to renew their treaty with you upon equitable terms if the Trustees are prepared to concede those points, which led to the abandonment of the former negotiations. It is now important that some decision should be formed as to the future plan of the Company in reference to their Station and Depots and I trust that the readiness with which the Directors consented under peculiar circumstances to the very high price proposed for the ground on behalf of the Trustees may not be converted into a motive for requiring other and more onerous conditions to which their duty must preclude them from assenting.[45]

This is an interesting letter. Firstly it seems that the agreement confirmed on 16 February was reneged upon – no reason is given but possibly the difficulties, whatever they were, are alluded to in Gibbs' diary for 23 April 1836.[46] Secondly the alternative site, 'which had already been offered'. Exactly what had been offered, by whom and where is a mystery. It is also clear from the letter that the company did try to get their Bill for the extension through Parliament in the 1836 Session.

40. The Local Act.

41. Lord Hill's Bridge.

42. This is left blank and the letter untraced.

43. Paddington Vestry Minutes, op.cit., 4/2/1837.

44. PRO RAIL 250/83, Abstract of Minutes, London Committee, Vol.3 p.10, 16/2/1837.

45. PRO RAIL 250/87, General Letter Book, London Committee, 11/7/1836.

46. Simmons, op.cit., p.21.

47. No copy of the lease seems to have survived in the records and archives of the GWR. However a registered copy of the lease dated 9 April 1851 is in the archives of the Church Commissioners and I am grateful to them for supplying me with a photocopy. The lease was surrendered in 1888 and followed by a lease dated 12 December 1888. The Counterpart of this lease is on permanent loan to the Guildhall Library, City of London.

48. PRO RAIL 250/87, General Letter Book 1835–6, 18/7/1836. Refer also to FIG.8, George Gutch's Map of Paddington 1828, and FIG.10, the Parliamentary Deposited Plan.

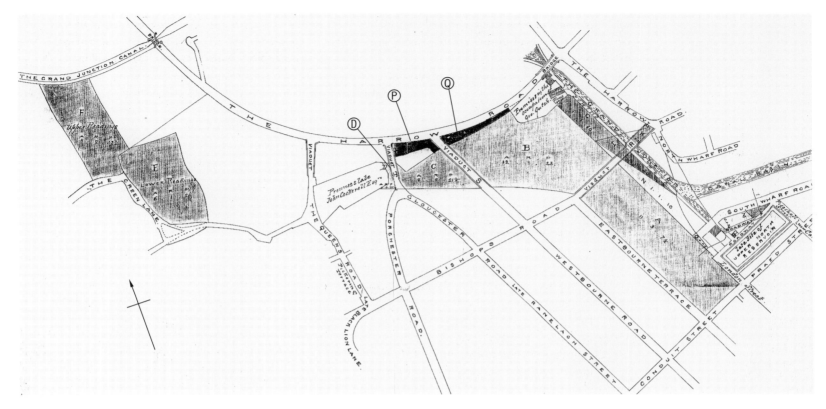

Another letter followed on 18 July, accompanied by a plan, supplied by Gutch, which had been annotated to show the precise measurement and location of the land for which the Company were willing to take a lease. This plan has not survived but it must be the same as that attached to the lease (FIG.9), which grants the land on a term of 99 years from 3 September 1837.[47] The letter describes the various plots:

> The portion in yellow contiguous to the Red Lion Public House is merely applicable to the purpose of an access for the line of Railway to the Depot.[48]

These are the approaches to the terminus, corresponding to areas C and D on the lease plan (FIG.9).

> The portion coloured brown to the eastward of the street called the Westbourne Road will comprise both the depot at the upper end and a line of approach, at the lower end, leaving a frontage to the Harrow Road on the north and to the Westbourne Road on the west.

This corresponds to area B on the lease plan (FIG.9).

> The portion coloured blue represents the spot for the principal depot for passengers adjoining the land which belongs to the Grand Junction Canal Co.

This corresponds to area A on the lease plan (FIG.9).

The original intention of the Company, to build the main passenger terminus on area A and the goods station on area B, had to be shelved for reasons of economy, and in fact the original terminus was always considered a temporary group of buildings, as was the goods depot which occupied the north-west portion of area A. This is clearly stated in the

9. Plan, forming part of a Lease dated 9 April 1851. Probably by George Gutch. See text for explanation of the letters. (Church Commissioners)

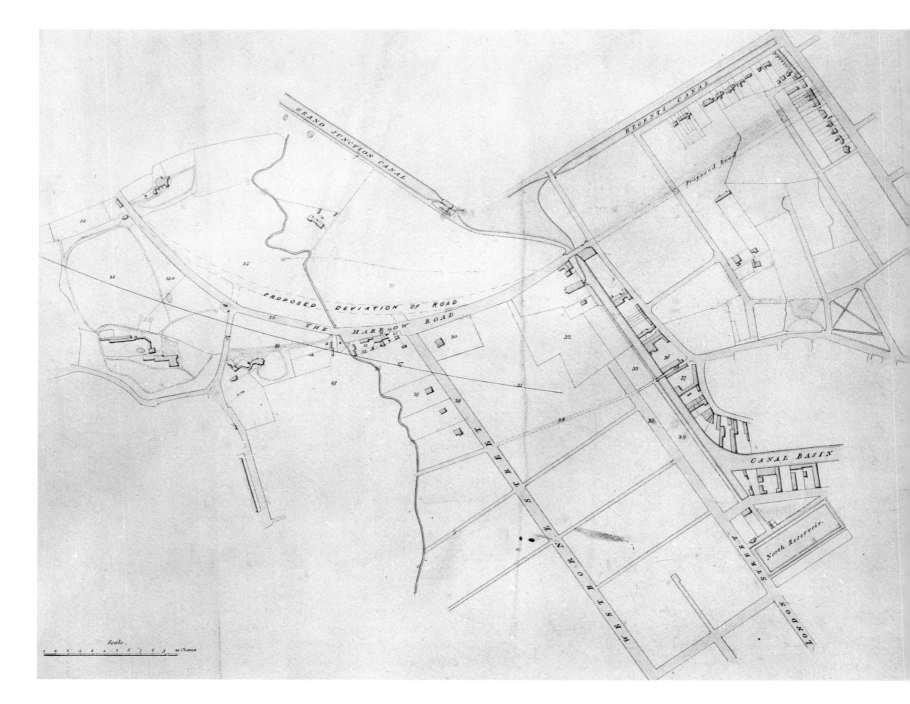

20 – PADDINGTON STATION 1833–1854

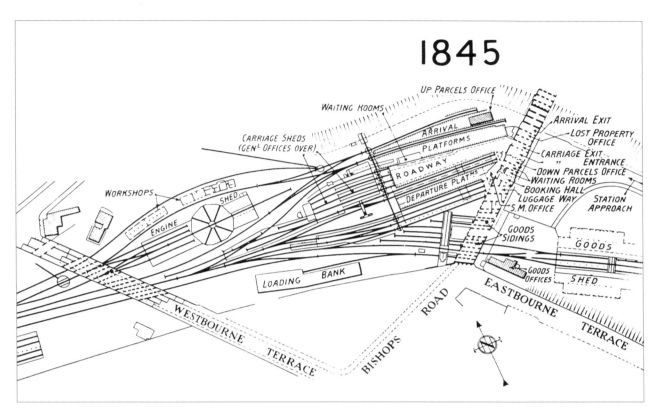

1845

Labels on plan: UP PARCELS OFFICE · WAITING ROOMS · ARRIVAL EXIT · LOST PROPERTY OFFICE · CARRIAGE EXIT ENTRANCE · ARRIVAL PLATFORMS · ROADWAY · DOWN PARCELS OFFICE · WAITING ROOMS · BOOKING HALL · LUGGAGE WAY · DEPARTURE PLATFMS · S.M. OFFICE · STATION APPROACH · CARRIAGE SHEDS (GENL OFFICES OVER) · WORKSHOPS · ENGINE SHED · LOADING BANK · GOODS SIDINGS · GOODS OFFICES · GOODS SHED · GOODS · WESTBOURNE TERRACE · BISHOPS ROAD · EASTBOURNE TERRACE

10 (far left). Parliamentary Deposited Plan, November 1836. Enlarged part, Paddington. This shows the proposed alteration to the Harrow Road. See also Appendix A. (London Metropolitan Archives)

11 (left). Plan of Paddington Station in 1845. This is a redrawn plan based on the original shown in FIG.13, it originally appeared in MacDermot (note 1) and subsequently in the Railway Gazette Supplement of August 1935. (This copy supplied by The Railway Club)

Directors' report to the 4th half-yearly general meeting of shareholders, held on 31 August 1837:

> The space allotted for the Depot in London, for Goods, will for the present be employed as a Temporary Station for Passengers until the permanent buildings can be erected . . .[49]

This was reaffirmed at the 11th meeting on 25 February 1841:

> It is still the opinion of the Directors that they ought to postpone as long as possible any disbursements for permanent building at their London Terminus making in the meantime the best use they can of the present Paddington Station deferring all consideration of the scale and extent of such buildings and consequently the provision of funds for them until the requirements of the traffic shall both compel and justify the outlay.[50]

So the passenger station was built on the site of the goods depot and the goods depot built on the site of the passenger station. Returning to the descriptions in the letter dated 18 July 1836:

> It is proposed to build a carriage bridge across the canal, instead of the present footway and the Directors will not object to incur the expense of making a proper carriage road in a direct line from the Bishop's Path and also to constitute a frontage for the property in that direction.

49. PRO RAIL 250/64, General Meetings of Proprietors Oct.1835 to Aug.1844, 31/8/1837.

50. Ibid., 25/2/1841.

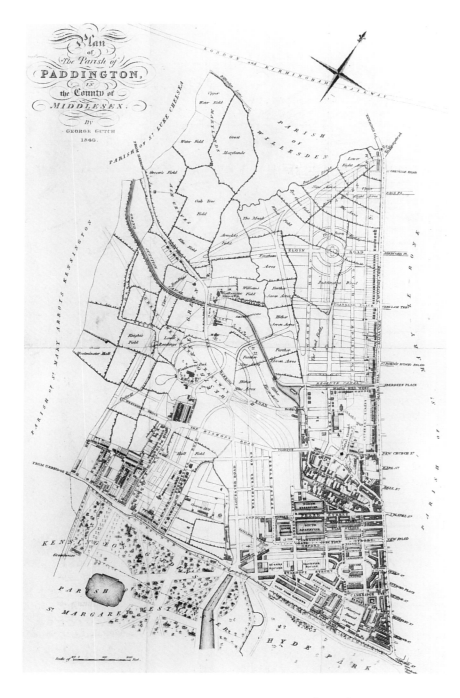

The new Bishop's Bridge became the main frontage to the temporary passenger terminus with the main entrance, booking office and other offices contained within its arches (FIG.11).

The Company propose to make an entrance to their Depot coloured brown by a road from the Harrow Road, near Mr Gutch's house.

This refers to areas P and Q on the lease plan (FIG.9).

The portion marked blue to be taken into possession by the Directors as soon as the notice to the present tenants that the land is required for building purposes can enable the Trustees of the Paddington Estate to give up the property.[51]

Finally, there were two fields (not within the area of this study) known as the Upper and Lower Readings, areas E and F.

The total area amounted to just over 44¾ acres for which the Great Western Railway paid an initial sum of £30,000 and an annual rent of £2,366.12s. The Bishop of London and Trustees of the Paddington Estate decided not to dispose of their freehold interest in the land and the Great Western Railway never held the freehold of the ground on which their London Terminus stood.[52] The price for the land purchased from the Grand Junction Canal Company was £24,109; there are no details of these negotiations in the archives of the Great Western Railway.

12. **Plan of the Parish of Paddington. George Gutch, 1840 This plan is not referred to in the text but is included as a comparison to FIG.8. It shows the railway terminating at Bishop's Bridge with the area to the south, between the bridge and Conduit (now Praed) Street, left as a blank, undeveloped, space. (Guildhall Library, Corporation of London)**

51. See APPENDIX A.

52. In 1958 the Church Commissioners, to whom the estates of the Bishops of London passed in the middle of the 19th century, sold their freehold interest in the site to the then British Transport Commission.

FIVE

Construction

IN NOVEMBER 1836 Brunel reported to the Board that, all the arrangements for obtaining possession of the land for the extension to Paddington having been completed, it was now necessary immediately to decide in what way the Company wished to carry out the work of constructing the line and terminus: whether by contractor after publicly advertising for tenders, by private contract, or by the Company acting as its own contractor.

> . . . The peculiar circumstances under which the company has obtained the power to commence the works upon their lands. . .

Brunel continues in his report,

> . . . the necessity of proceeding with great precaution in many circumstances to prevent causes of complaint from the neighbouring land owners and the possibility of being occasionally obliged to interrupt or delay the works . . .[53]

A contractor would have to allow sufficient profit margin to cover all the many conditions which would have to be written into any contract, and thus raise the price so much that the Company could execute the work themselves for less. (All this was occasioned, of course, by the Company wishing to commence the work before obtaining the Act.) Brunel goes on to state that where the earthworks were concerned there was no alternative, and the Company should undertake the work itself with directly-employed labour; however, the brickwork could be let in sections or lots to local influential builders. An assistant engineer would have to be appointed to supervise the earthworks and the Company would have to buy in a temporary stock of rails, wagons and plant, for an estimate or limited cost of £8,000.

Brunel pre-empted any decision by the Board by having already taken steps to obtain tenders for the supply of rails, timber and iron, and making arrangements for Robert Archibald to act as assistant engineer.[54] There is an estimate in Brunel's private letterbook for the period October 1836 to April 1837 and headed 'Great Western Railway Extension' (see APPENDIX C) which perhaps indicates his decision to forge ahead.[55]

Although, according to Gibb's diary, work on the section between Acton and Paddington would not start until approval had been given by the shareholders at the August 1837 meeting,[56] work in fact began in April 1837 with preliminary earthworks, some £450 being paid out in wages during that month. The Company decided to carry out these works in exactly the way that Brunel suggested, becoming its own contractor for the major earthworks and laying the permanent way. The bulk of the brickwork was let to Messrs Grissell & Peto and Messrs B.&N. Sherwood, both in Brunel's opinion being 'highly respectable brick layers and excellent workmen'.[57] Construction continued to the end of 1845, which, in spite of the major and permanent earthworks, bridges and alterations to several roads, was a considerable period of time.

Construction of the terminus is not well chronicled either in the minutes or letterbooks of the Company; however, there is much information in the Company's account books. There are seven separate accounts in the ledgers and journals which chronicle the construction of the terminus: Paddington Terminus, Paddington Station, Paddington Stables, Paddington Merchandise Station, Paddington Engine House, Paddington

53. PRO RAIL 250/82, I.K. Brunel's Reports to the Board of Directors, 9/11/1836.

54. Ibid.

55. University of Bristol, Brunel Collection and Archive, Letterbook 2.

56. Simmons, op.cit., p.23.

57. PRO RAIL 250/82, I.K. Brunel's Reports to the Board of Directors, 6/7/1837.

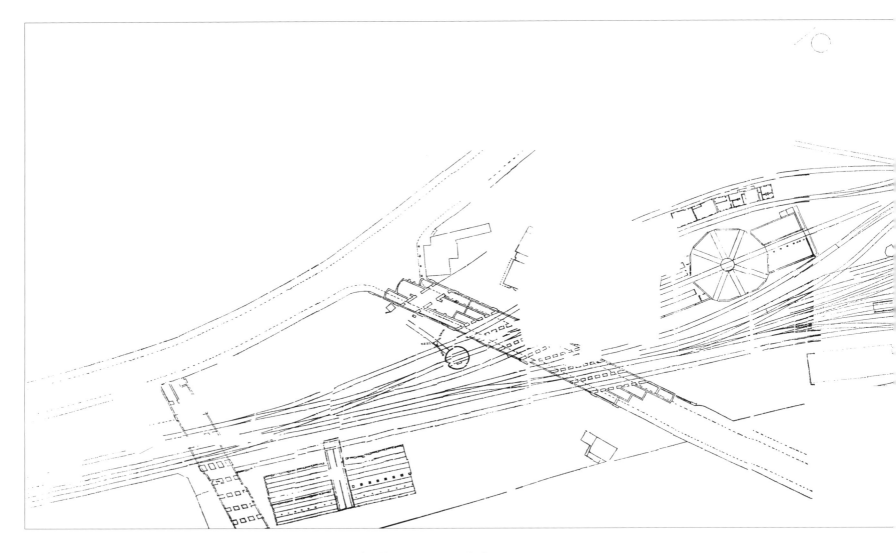

13. Plan of Paddington Station, as built, *c.*1852.
This and FIGS 14 to 16 are reproduced from original drawings formerly held in the Chief Engineer's Plan Office, Paddington (moved to Swindon in the early 80s). The reason for dating the drawing to 1852 is the 'Catalogue of Registered Plans and Drawings 1834–1880 at Paddington' (PRO 253/1). Under the reference number 6245, which is written on the drawing, although not shown here, is the entry: 'Paddington Terminus General Plan 1852'. 1852 is not necessarily the date the plan was drawn and it is almost certainly the original from which FIG.11 was redrawn. (Railtrack Great Western – see Preface)

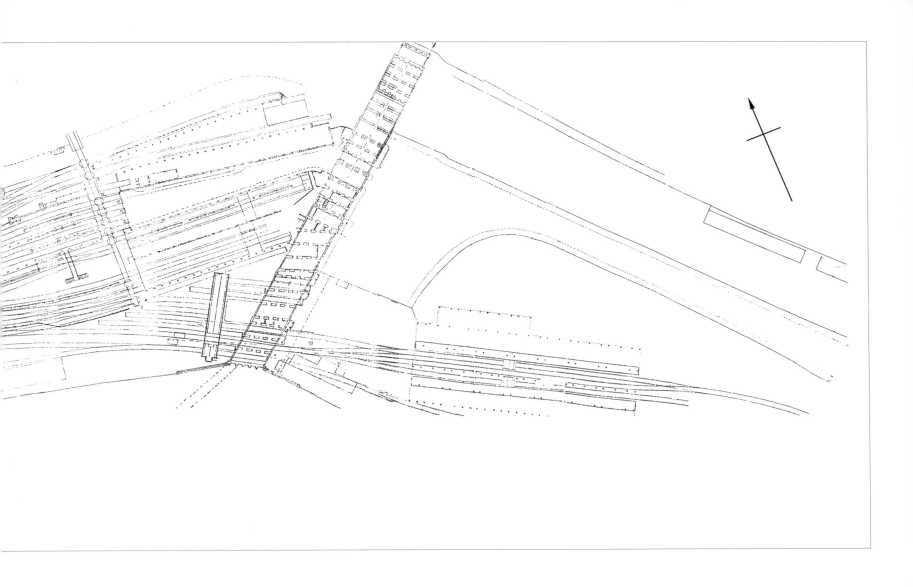

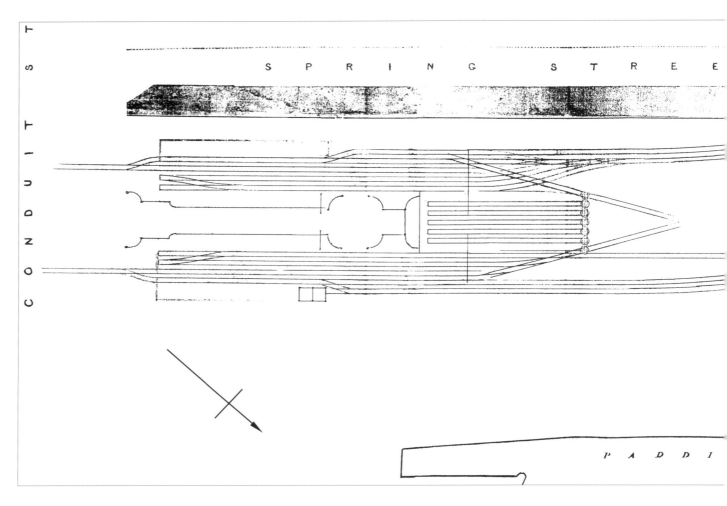

58. PRO RAIL 250/64, 6th Half
Yearly General Meeting, 15/8/1838.

59. R.B. Wilson (ed.) *Sir Daniel
Gooch – Memoirs and Diary,* 1972
'I left Manchester and went to
London, beginning my duties with
the Great Western Railway on the
18th August 1837 . . . My first work
was to prepare plans for the engine
houses at Paddington and
Maidenhead . . .' pp.27–28.

Carriage Station and Paddington New Offices (over the carriage shed). These accounts, from April 1837 to the end of 1845, are summarised in APPENDIX B. In addition there are separate accounts for the land of each landowner, the main ones being the Grand Junction Canal Company and the Paddington Estate. Permanent way has also not been included in Appendix B as this was debited to a separate account for the whole line.

Paddington Terminus account is assumed to cover the major earthworks, brickwork for bridges and viaducts, retaining walls, sewers and drains, and the roads which the Company had contracted with the Paddington Estate to make. The Paddington Station account includes the departure and arrival platforms, waiting rooms, booking and general offices. Paddington Merchandise Station is the goods depot and Paddington Carriage Station is the carriage shed. Stables, Engine House and New Offices are self explanatory. The cost of each of these is given in TABLE I.

The total of £231,619 compares well with the estimate dated August 1838,[58] reproduced in APPENDIX C. If the

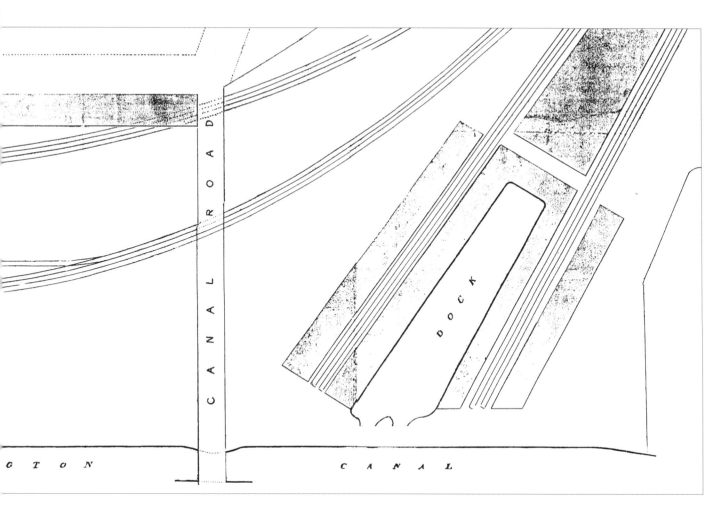

14. Early Terminus Plan,
pre-August 1837.
Possibly by I.K. Brunel.
This drawing shows a plan for
the terminus on its original site,
Conduit and Spring Streets
are now Praed Street and
Eastbourne Terrace respectively.
Canal Road is Bishop's Bridge
Road. (Railtrack Great Western
– see Preface)

figures for land and permanent way are deducted from the total, this gives an estimate of £234,046.

The figure of £1,788 for the engine shed appears low. This building was to the design of Daniel Gooch[59] and comparable in size to the goods shed and some of the cost may have been posted to the wrong account.

The accounts make it possible to examine the chronology of construction. Work on the major earthworks and brickworks started on 22 April 1837 (the Act was finally obtained on 3 July 1837) and continued until the end of the year,

Table 1: Construction Costs	
Paddington Terminus	£189,997
Paddington Station	13,181
Paddington Stables	3,292
Paddington Merchandise Station	9,773
Paddington Engine House	1,788
Paddington Carriage Station	9,831
Paddington New Offices	3,757
total	£231,619

with £36,870 being spent on wages for the earthworks, and £30,030 going to the two main contractors for the brick-work. In addition expenditure on the temporary rails and plant for carrying out the earthworks amounted to £7,405, compared with Brunel's estimate of £8,000.

Work continued throughout 1838 and 1839 with £33,903 and £36,381 being spent on wages and brickwork respective-ly. In August and September 1839 work on the formation of roads commenced, including the diverted part of the Harrow Road. Work on the passenger station started in September 1838, followed by the stables in November of the same year, the goods station in October 1839 and the engine house in September 1839. During the years 1840 and 1841 expendi-ture on wages dwindled to £2,103 indicating that the earth-works were nearing completion, but some brickwork and work on the formation of roads was still being carried out. Work on the passenger station, engine house, goods station and stables continued throughout 1840/41 and work on the carriage station started in July 1840. There is no expenditure on wages shown after the end of 1841, indicating that the workforce employed by the Company had been dismissed or transferred to other contracts elsewhere on the line, the work having been completed. However, during 1842 and 1843 there was some small expenditure on brickwork and roads. Also work continued on the passenger station, goods station and carriage shed.

It had been decided at a Board meeting on 19 March 1842 to make improvements to the arrival lines and platforms, and provide a waiting room for an estimated £2,460. There is also mention of recent additions to the goods depot:

> That the said plans be approved and the works be commenced forthwith under contract upon schedule prices not exceeding those of the recent additions to the Goods Shed.[60]

At a later meeting on 8 April 1842, a plan for roofing over the whole space between the arrival platforms, instead of the par-tial roof originally projected, was put before the Board at an estimate of £475, and duly approved.[61]

The passenger station was finished in December 1844 and the carriage and goods stations were both finished towards the end of 1845. At a meeting on 4 March 1843, Brunel sub-mitted to the Board a plan of a building, to be erected over the carriage shed to provide additional offices, as early as October 1841. A report by the Chairman and Deputy Chair-man mentions insufficient space and accommodation for var-ious accounting and administrative functions.[62] The estimate for this building was £2,400 and work started in August 1843, the final cost being £3,757.

As mentioned above, due to economy, the passenger sta-tion was built on the site of the eventual goods depot and vice versa. However, Brunel did produce at least one early plan for a terminus to occupy the intended original site (FIG.14). This shows a building of approximately 260ft frontage to Conduit Street, now Praed Street. The station is divided, into departure side, to the south west, alongside Spring Street (Eastbourne Terrace) and arrival side, by a central roadway which leads to a central area, presumably containing booking office, waiting rooms and other offices. There are two plat-form faces to each side with two spare lines between each giv-ing a total of four lines each side. There is an extra platform face in each side of the station gained by the main face being stepped back, about half-way along to afford space for an extra running line. The approaches consist of four lines which split just beyond Westbourne Bridge – two lines to each side of the station. One line from each of the two sides extends beyond the station building as far as Conduit Street. Behind the central building is the carriage shed with seven turntables affording access to five sidings. The goods station is intriguing, as it is obvious that it was originally intended to construct a large dock connected to the Paddington Canal, as part of a transfer depot between canal and railway. This drawing seems to date to before 31 August 1837, the date on which it was decided to build only a temporary station.

The next plan for the terminus (FIG.15) shows a diminu-tive station tucked away in the south-west corner of the site and completely dwarfed by the goods depot, which remains unaltered – it is almost as if the passenger terminus has been

60. PRO RAIL 250/3, Board Minutes 19/3/1842.

61. Ibid., 8/4/1842.

62. PRO RAIL 250/2, Board Minutes 5/10/1841.

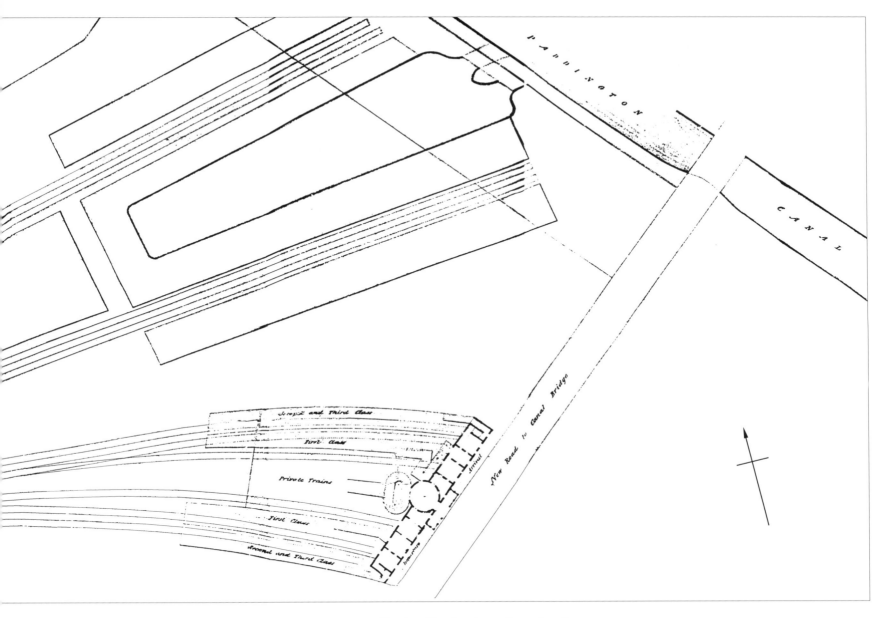

Within the plan image, the following labels appear:

PADDINGTON

CANAL

Second and Third Class
First Class
Private Trains
Arrival
First Class
Second and Third Class

New Road to Canal Bridge

15. Terminus Plan circa August/September 1837.
This curious plan seems to be drawn to the wrong scale, a separate building fronts the platforms, divided into departure
and arrival sides with between a grand circular entrance to the central part of the station reserved for private trains.
(Railtrack Great Western — see Preface)

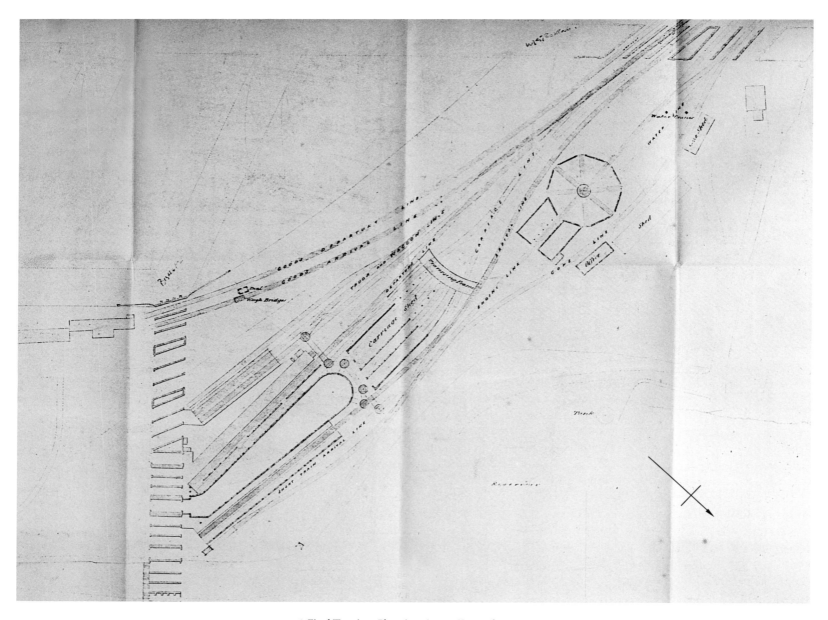

16. Final Terminus Plan circa August/September 1837.
This scheme utilises the viaduct carrying the Bishop's Walk, renamed Bishop's Bridge, over the site
as a frontage for the station and incorporating various entrances, exits and offices.
(Railtrack Great Western see Preface)

drawn to the wrong scale. The plan shows a somewhat fancy building fronting separate platforms for second- and third-class, first-class and private trains.

The final proposal for the terminus (FIG.16) shows a group of buildings utilising the proposed viaduct carrying the Bishop's Road over the site, as a frontage for the station. This viaduct effectively cut the whole site in two. However, as we have seen, it was an express condition of the agreement with the Parish of Paddington and the Bishop of London and the Trustees of the Paddington Estate that this ancient right of way should be preserved and improved to form a roadway. The station is again divided into an arrival and departure building separated by a roadway which enters through one of the arches of the viaduct. The roadway runs down the whole length of the passenger station to a sweeping semi-circle behind which is the carriage shed. As well as the main entrance, various offices are contained within the other arches of the viaduct. The idea of a large dock attached to the canal has been abandoned. The goods depot is not shown on this plan, apart from the approaches and the goods offices in the south-west corner at the apex of Bishop's Bridge and Westbourne Terrace.

The terminus as built is shown in FIGS 11 and 13 which show it in 1845 and 1852 respectively. The plans are identical and therefore no major alterations or additions were carried out within this period. The sweeping curve at the end of the roadway was not carried out – the end being simply squared off. There is an extra carriage shed immediately out-

17. Lithograph. 'Paddington Station' by J.C. Bourne, from his *History and Description of the Great Western Railway*, 1846. View looking north west, Bourne has worked up his sketches to produce a grand vista – almost certainly grander than the reality of the day.

18. Anonymous sketch, looking west towards Eastbourne Terrace. The low building with the hipped roofs is the Goods Office and the taller building on the extreme left, only partly in the picture, is the Goods Shed. (City of Westminster Archives Centre)

19. Water-colour, by Bailey Sherwood, possibly the B. Sherwood of B.&N. Sherwood, one of the principal brickwork contractors (p.23). View looking north-east across the goods yard to the canal and the village of Paddington beyond, the church in the distance is St Mary's. (City of Westminster Archives Centre)

20. **Anonymous Sketch, looking towards Eastbourne Terrace. Compare with FIG.11. (City of Westminster Archives Centre)**

side the departure side and the engine shed is much bigger, with a larger west-facing arm.

The appearance of this group of buildings would have been plain and simple:

> The Committee resolve that it is their opinion that the greatest economy should be observed in construction of the Depot and that no architectural ornament involving unnecessary expense be adopted.[63]

Bourne, however, has managed to make the frontage appear quite grand in the illustration of the terminus in his 'History and Description of the Great Western Railway'[64] (FIG.17), while Biddle[65] attributes to Brunel the first ever use of ornamental valancing on the platform awnings.

Other illustrations of the exterior of the station show a less grand appearance. The watercolour (FIG.19) by Mr Bailey Sherwood, one of the two principal contractors, gives a view of the goods yard and entrance roadway from Eastbourne Terrace across to the canal and the Harrow Road. In the left foreground are the goods offices and to the right the goods depot. This illustration shows a more restrained Bishop's Bridge more in keeping with the above resolution.

An anonymous sketch (FIG.20) shows the opposite view, towards Eastbourne Terrace – the squat building occupying the middle ground is the goods office, which seems to be a masonry building with leaded windows. Another sketch (FIG.18) from the same viewpoint, but from a lower level, shows a timber building – the sketch is probably a study for

63. PRO RAIL 250/83, Abstract of Minutes, London Committee. Vol.3, p.35.

64 John C. Bourne, *History and Description of the Great Western Railway*. David Bogue, London 1846. Reprinted in facsimile edition, with some omissions, David & Charles, Newton Abbot, 1970.

65. G. Biddle, *Victorian Stations*, 1973.

21. Interior of the Station. Woodcut from *The Illustrated London News* 22 July 1843. The only known view of the interior, the scene depicts an arrival, the building in the right foreground is the Up Parcels Office with the embankment beyond – see FIG.11.

66. *Paddington 1854–1979*, British Rail, Western Region, 1979.

The illustration on page 2 of this book, the official history of Paddington Station for the 125th anniversary, which purports to be the: 'Interior of the original Paddington station taken from a contemporary print' is most certainly not the original station.

67. Westminster Fire Office, Minute Book 29/4/1841 and 7/10/1841. City of Westminster Archives Centre.

68. Paddington Vestry Minutes, 2/5/1837, 7/6/1842 and *passim*.

69. Ibid., 1/2/1848 and 7/3/1848.

a woodcut (*shown on the back cover*). The treatment of the Prince of Wales Hotel in Eastbourne Terrace in these various studies is interesting; that in FIG.20 seem to be the more convincing, whereas the originator of FIG.18 seems to be more concerned with station activities.

The only known illustration of the interior of the station[66] is the woodcut from *The Illustrated London News* for 22 July 1843 (FIG.21) which shows a king-strut tie-beam truss roof with twin-angle struts, carried on slender, fluted, cast-iron columns with splayed capitals. The illustration depicts an arrival – the crowd walking away from the train, the lady on the extreme left getting into, rather than alighting from, the road carriage, and the arrow on the 'Way Out' sign, although not visible, pointing out of the picture, towards Bishop's Bridge. The building in the right foreground, therefore, is the up-parcels office (see FIG.11) and that in the background, at the Bristol or west end of the platform, is possibly the arrival waiting room.

In April 1841 the Company applied to the Westminster Fire Office for cover for the buildings at Paddington. After a survey the insurance company declined to cover the arrival and departure sheds, the carriage shed and the engine house for more than £10,000, while the limit on the goods shed was £5,000. Considering the cost of these buildings it is possible that the Westminster Fire Office considered the risk of fire too great to cover the buildings to their true value.[67]

Throughout the late 1830s and early 1840s there was a great deal of correspondence between the Vestry and the Company concerning repairs to, and the state of, the parish roads. There was a delay in finishing the Bishop's Bridge, particularly that part which spanned the canal, and this led to a large number of complaints from local traders and inhabitants. All this culminated in various court proceedings which were eventually settled out of court.[68] The vestry also experienced difficulties in assessing and collecting rates from the Company and this was eventually settled by arbitration.[69] The rateable values for the years 1844, 1845 and 1846 were £6,215, £7,290 and £7,378 respectively.

SIX

The Station at Work

THE FIRST TRAIN from London to Maidenhead, a directors' special with invited guests, left Paddington at 11.30am on 31 May 1838. Four days later on 4 June the line officially opened to the public, some 8 months after Brunel's promised opening date. Gibbs records in his diary that they carried 1,479 people, and that receipts amounted to £226.[70]

Before considering the station at work it is worth recording that when trains first started running there was no station at Paddington to speak of. Most of the facilities would have been contained within the arches of Bishop's Bridge, but even this was probably incomplete – the Company having agreed to construct the roads and bridges within 18 months of the passing of the Act on 3 July 1837. Work on the passenger station buildings proper did not start until September 1838, and what temporary facilities, if any, were supplied for the comfort and convenience of passengers is not known. Railway travel was of course in its very infancy, and most customers would have known no better – however, the situation at Paddington seems exceptional, even for the standards of the time.

The *Morning Chronicle* for 6 June carried an advertisement for eight trains each way, Monday to Saturday, advertised to depart at 8, 9 and 10am, 12 noon, 4, 5, 6 and 7pm, and six trains on Sundays to depart at 7, 8 and 9am, and 5, 6 and 7pm. The fares are given in TABLE 2. A similar advertisement appeared in *The Times* for 2 June (FIG.22). Some 10,360 people passed through the terminus in the first week, up to the evening of Sunday 10 June.[71]

During the first two-and-a-half years of operation, up to December 1840, the Company did not issue a proper timetable, largely due to the first batch of locomotives that worked the line being extremely unreliable:

> At the opening in 1838 we found the engines were so inefficient that time-table working was hopeless; one or two engines might keep time, the other eight or ten were always out of time. So we suspended time-tables till the locomotive power became sufficient.[72]

MacDermot describes the situation thus:

> It may be safely stated, without exaggeration, that in the whole history of British railways there has never existed such an extraordinary collection of freak locomotives as those which were built for the Great Western and delivered during a period of about eighteen months from November 1837.[73]

Table 2: Fares from Paddington				
	FIRST CLASS		SECOND CLASS	
	Posting Carriage	Passenger Coach	Coach	Open Carriage
West Drayton	4s 0d	3s 6d	2s 0d	1s 6d
Slough	5s 6d	4s 6d	3s 0d	2s 6d
Maidenhead	6s 6d	5s 6d	4s 0d	3s 6d

70. Simmons, op.cit., p.38.

71. Ibid., entry for 16 June 1838, p.39.

72. Charles Saunders, evidence to the Parliamentary Committee on Railways, April 1841. Quoted in MacDermot, op. cit., p.329.

73. Ibid., p.372.

GREAT WESTERN RAILWAY.—The public are informed that this RAILWAY will be OPENED for the CONVEYANCE of PASSENGERS only between London, West Drayton, Slough, and Maidenhead station, on Monday, the 4th June. The following will be the times for the departure of trains each way, from London and from Maidenhead, (excepting on Sundays,) until further notice :—

Trains each way.

8 o'clock morning ; 4 o'clock afternoon.
9 o'clock ditto 5 o'clock ditto
10 o'clock ditto 6 o'clock ditto
12 o'clock noon 7 o'clock ditto

Trains on Sundays each way.

7 o'clock morning ; 5 o'clock afternoon.
8 o'clock ditto 6 o'clock ditto
9 o'clock ditto 7 o clock ditto

Each train will take up or set down passengers at West Drayton and Slough.

Fares of Passengers.

	First Class.		Second Class.	
	Posting Carriage.	Passenger Coach.	Coach.	Open Carriage.
	s. d.	s. d.	s. d.	s. d.
Paddington Station to West Drayton	4 0	3 6	2 0	1 6
to Slough	5 6	4 6	3 0	2 6
to Maidenhead	6 6	5 6	4 0	3 6

Notice is also given that on and after Monday, the 11th June, carriages and horses will be conveyed on the railway, and passengers and parcels booked for conveyance by coaches in connexion with the Railway Company to the west of England, including Stroud, Cheltenham, and Glocester, as well as to Oxford, Newbury, Reading, Henley, Marlow, Windsor, Uxbridge, and other contiguous places. By order of the Directors,

CHARLES A. SAUNDERS, } Secs.
THOMAS OSLER,

22. Advertisement from *The Times*, 2 June 1838.

74. The two exceptions, 'North Star' and 'Morning Star', were built by Robert Stephenson & Co., to the order of the 5'6" gauge New Orleans Railway. Because of financial problems experienced by that Railway the engines were not delivered and were purchased by the Great Western Railway after having been converted to the 7' gauge.

75. MacDermot, op. cit., p.329.

76. Ibid., p.333.

77. Reports by Seymour Clarke to Charles Saunders. Quoted in Ibid, p.331. Seymour Clarke was appointed to the post of Traffic Superintendent in June 1838, having formally been Brunel's chief clerk.

78. Ibid., p.365.

79. Ibid., p.364.

80. Ibid., p.368.

The blame for this situation must rest with Brunel since, although he did not design the locomotives, all but two of them were built to his specifications.[74] Brunel, unlike his father or his great friend and rival Robert Stephenson, was not a competent mechanical engineer and certainly could never be regarded as a locomotive engineer.

The train service was increased to nine trains each way later in 1838 with four 'short trains' being added to serve the stations at Ealing and Hanwell. By May 1839 another train had been added to Maidenhead and back, and a further intermediate station opened at Southall. The 'Train Bill' issued for the opening of this station is reproduced in FIG.23, 'Posting Carriage' fares advertised for the opening having now gone and the 'Second Class Close [coach]' fare taken out when the line was extended to Twyford on 1 July.[75] Following the opening to Twyford, goods traffic commenced, initially operated by carriers who also took third-class passengers.

The Company did not take these passengers until the line was opened to Reading on 30 March 1840 when it was announced that:

The Goods Train Passengers will be conveyed in uncovered trucks by the Goods Trains only . . .[76]

The line was extended to Faringdon Road on 20 July with nineteen trains each way including two goods trains, and extended to Wootton Bassett on 16 December 1840 when the first proper time-table was introduced. Mails began to be carried from 4 February 1840 with a night mail to and from Twyford. The line opened throughout to Bristol on 30 June 1841 – a time-table for 30 July showing 17 departures and 17 arrivals including two goods trains (FIGS 24 & 25).

It was possible, if one could afford it, to hire specials. One such instance, possibly one of the first, occurred on the 25 January 1839 when the Duke of Lucca arrived at Paddington in a hurry to get to Windsor. A locomotive and one six-wheeled carriage were provided for the journey to Slough. Seymour Clarke, the traffic superintendent, accompanied the Duke and his party and charged him £10 for the single journey – the Duke returning by scheduled train.[77]

It took Queen Victoria until 13 June 1842 to make up her mind to try railway travel, on this first occasion she travelled from Slough to Paddington. Very soon afterwards she gave up travelling to and from Windsor by road and used the line regularly. Although special facilities were provided for the Queen at Slough, which was a permanent building, no such facilities were provided at Paddington until permanent buildings were erected in 1854. The Queen was not the first reigning Monarch to use the railway however, the King of Prussia, Frederick William IV travelling from Paddington to Slough on 24 January 1842 to attend the christening of the Prince of Wales at Windsor.

Train working during the first months of the railway was alarmingly haphazard. Trains were not always confined to their proper Up or Down line and there were no fixed signals, the line being divided into 'beats' controlled by constables who gave signals with their arms to control trains. Locomotives were often sent out to look for late trains on the same line! Gooch in his memoirs recalls some thirty years later:

> When I look back upon that time, it is a marvel to me that we escaped serious accidents. It was no uncommon thing to take an engine out on the line to look for a late train that we expected and many times have I seen the train coming and reversed the engine and run back out of its way as quickly as I could.[78]

To add to all of this, various experimental trains were using the line. That of Dr Dionysios Lardner was travelling back and forth during September and October 1838 between the regular services and one of his pupils was killed in an accident on the line. Charles Babbage, a friend of Brunel was also allowed to perform experiments using trains on the line.[79]

The practice of trains regularly running on the wrong line continued until October 1840 when it was stopped. Sending locomotives to look for late trains continued into the 1870s, albeit in modified form – the engine ran on the proper line and having passed the train going in the opposite direction, ran on to the next crossing, returning to render any assistance necessary. One particularly unfortunate incident occurred on 2 April 1839 when an engine, which was returning to the depot, ran into the Engine House – the points being wrongly switched – completely destroying the eastern pair of doors, running into three standing locomotives and driving them out through the western doors, seriously damaging one of them. This happened to be one of the only two reliable ones! Apart from this incident and the death of Lardner's pupil further down the line there were no major accidents at Paddington and, despite the delays and frequent derailments, the complaints book kept at Paddington remained blank, at least until April 1839.[80] From about March 1840, the hand signals given by the constables gradually gave way to fixed disc-and-crossbar signals designed by Brunel, some of which remained in use until the end of the century.

23. Train Bill, May 1839. (MacDermot, 1927)

Great Western Railway.

ALTERATION OF TRAINS.
LONDON to CIRENCESTER, BATH, BRISTOL and BRIDGEWATER.

In compliance with directions received from Her Majesty's Postmaster General, for the conveyance of the Mails, the Trains on and after FRIDAY, the 30th July, will run as specified below:—

TIME TABLE.

(Detailed timetable of Down Trains and Up Trains, 10th August 1841.)

24. Time-Table, 30 July 1841. Recto. (MacDermot, 1927)

Another problem at Paddington in the early years was water supply – there was no mains supply to the site and water had to be brought in by tanker. Seymour Clarke in his report to Saunders for 8 January 1839 highlights the problem:

I have again been suffering for the want of a reserve water tank. No water came in during the night. We had enough for the 8 o'clock but the expected supply not having come by 9, I was obliged to get the fire engine out and had recourse to a little well near my cottage and by this means sent off the 9, 9.30 and 10 o'clock trains, taking those engines that had most in their tender. I now have men pumping the old saw pit . . .[81]

The tickets issued to passengers were of paper with counterfoils and these continued in use until at least August 1842. The tickets were stamped with the date and time of the train and the passenger's destination. After booking, the passenger proceeded to the train and gave the ticket to the conductor, who was travelling inspector and guard rolled into one and had complete charge of the train including the engine crew. The passenger was shown to the carriage or compartment appropriate to this destination and locked in. The booking clerk made up a way-bill or passenger list from his counterfoils, which listed the number of passengers for each station. At exactly what point the clerk stopped selling tickets before a train was due to depart is not clear, but he had to deliver the way-bill to the conductor before the train could proceed. At intermediate stations the station clerk would add his own passengers and their destinations to the way-bill, whilst the conductor unlocked the relevant doors for passengers alighting at that particular station. Having done that he would then have to unlock the relevant doors for those passengers joining the train. All in all a somewhat cumbersome procedure which remained in force for some years. Children were at first carried free, then charged for and then again, from April 1839, carried free up to the age of three, and half price between three and ten years. The practice of locking passengers in continued until June 1842 when the Company, reluctantly, dropped the practice following instructions from the Board

DOWN TRAINS leave PADDINGTON STATION, all calling at Slough, Reading, Steventon, Swindon, and Chippenham Stations.

UP TRAINS, all calling at Chippenham, Swindon, Steventon, Reading, and Slough Stations.

SHORT TRAINS DOWN.
Calling at Intermediate Stations, as per Train Bill.

SHORT TRAINS UP TO PADDINGTON,
Calling at Intermediate Stations, as per Train Bill.

FARES.

DOWN from CIRENCESTER.

UP to CIRENCESTER.

25. Time-Table, 30 July 1841. Verso. (MacDermot, 1927)

---

of Trade, after a terrible accident in France in which 53 passengers were burnt to death.[82]

Each first-class passenger was allowed 112lb of luggage free of charge and each second-class passenger 56lb. All luggage unless booked and paid for separately was carried at the passenger's own risk. There were specific arrangements for dealing with luggage at Paddington. The 1848 Rule Book specifies:

> All articles of London luggage not taken charge of by the passengers themselves are to have red labels pasted on showing the initial letter of the owner's surname, and the porters at Paddington are, on the arrival of the trains, to take care that the luggage thus labelled is placed in the proper bins or divisions of

the barrier on the platforms, and delivered only to the proper owners.[83]

Early in 1843 a sub-committee was formed to consider economies and cost cutting which could be adopted without impairing the quality of service; one such economy was a reduction in the number of personnel. In order to do this a census of staff was taken which records 213 employed at Paddington. In addition there were four conductors, 42 passenger guards and ten goods guards giving a total of 269.[84] Among these would have been Mary Coulsell, the first woman employed by the Company, appointed by the Directors on 25 May 1838 as 'Female Attendant at Paddington'.[85]

A particularly important development which took place at

81. Ibid., p.329.

82. Ibid., p.367–69.

83. Ibid., p.357.

84. PRO RAIL 250/3, Board Minutes, 14/2/1843.

85. MacDermot, op. cit., p.357.

Paddington during 1839 was the installation of an electric telegraph between the Terminus and West Drayton. The first practical telegraph in England was patented by William Fothergill Cooke and Professor Charles Wheatstone in 1837. Cooke had made experiments, late in 1836, on the Liverpool & Manchester Railway in the Lime Street Tunnel where there were problems with signalling. The Liverpool & Manchester were impressed but had already committed themselves to a pneumatic system. Early in 1837 Cooke met Wheatstone, both men having secured introductions to the London & Birmingham Railway. Later in the year the two men formed a partnership[86] and commenced experiments on the London & Birmingham between Camden Town and Euston. Stephenson was much impressed with the telegraph but was unable to convince his Board of Directors. Engineers and directors from other companies had been invited to attend some of the experiments. Among these was Brunel who immediately put the proposition before his Board; since he was more persuasive, an agreement was drawn up in April 1838 to cover the laying of the telegraph alongside the first section of line, from Paddington to West Drayton. The agreement was confirmed on 24 May 1838 with a proviso that it should be extended to Maidenhead if successful.

Cooke was employed as contractor to lay and install the telegraph which consisted of six wires insulated with cotton and varnish. It was Cooke's idea to lay the wires in timber troughs alongside the line, but Brunel specified that they should be threaded through iron pipes and attached to short posts at the side of the line, to afford better protection against accidental damage and vandalism.[87] The pipes used were gas pipes of 3/4 inch internal diameter supplied by Russell Gas Tube Manufacture Co., of Wednesbury, Staffordshire.[88] The telegraph was in use as far as Hanwell by April 1839 and completed to West Drayton in July 1839. The telegraph was used for general messages and for conveying intelligence on the passing of trains, but was not used for signalling and was therefore not essential for the running of trains. It was the first working telegraph in daily use over a fairly long distance and caused something of a sensation in London, the Duke of Wellington and other notables going to see it in use on 24 August 1839:

> Sims and I received the Duke of Wellington at Paddington and showed him the Electro-Magnetic Telegraph and the station.[89]

After a year or so of working, the wires became damaged and the system fell out of use. Cooke had hoped that the telegraph could be extended to Bristol and Brunel submitted extension proposals to a general meeting of shareholders in 1842, but they were not passed due to costs and doubts over profitable return.[90] To prevent the complete dismantling of the system, Cooke put forward a proposition that the telegraph should be put in order and operated by him at his own expense. This was considered by the Board at a meeting at Steventon on 6 October 1842[91] and confirmed at a meeting at Bristol on 10 January 1843. It was at this meeting that the Board recommended that all future meetings, including committees, should be held at Paddington, thus endowing Paddington with the status of Headquarters of the Company.[92]

Cooke's proposals allowed for public use of the telegraph, with continued free use by the Company – until then it had been confined exclusively to railway use. He also gave up Brunel's idea of iron tubes, instead suspending the wires from iron poles, approximately 10 to 12 feet in height and 150 feet apart. These were the first such telegraph poles with the wires insulated from the poles by glass or pottery insulators. The new system was opened between Paddington and Slough in 1843 and visitors were charged one shilling admission to see the 'marvel of science'.[93] Thomas Howe was the first licensee to work the telegraph at an annual rental of £170.

Cooke and Wheatstone's patents were bought up by the Electric Telegraph Company in 1846, shortly after it was incorporated; the partnership had by then broken up. Following a dispute with the GWR in May 1848 over damage to an engine, the Electric Telegraph Co. removed the system in June 1849 saying that it was not remunerative and had not covered its maintenance expenses.[94] However, by 1852 the telegraph had been reinstated between Paddington and Bristol.

86. Cooke, who had had some scientific and technical education, was the commercial and business half, whilst Wheatstone, who was appointed professor of experimental philosophy at King's College, London, in 1834, and was elected a Fellow of the Royal Society in 1836, formed the scientific half of the partnership.

87. MacDermot, op. cit., p.325.

88. F. Celoria, 'Early Victorian Telegraphs in London's Topography, History and Archaeology', in, London & Middlesex Archaeological Society, *Collectanea Londiniensia*, 1978, p.425.

89. Simmons, op. cit., p.70. Sims was a fellow director. See also Seymour Clarke to Saunders, 24/8/1839, quoted in MacDermot, op. cit., p.326.

90. J. Kieve, *The Electric Telegraph*, 1973.

91. PRO RAIL 250/3, Board Minutes, 6/10/1842.

92. Ibid., 10/1/1843.

93. J. Kieve, op. cit.

94. Ibid.

SEVEN

Conclusion

As the Great Western Railway extended further afield, the facilities at the temporary terminus at Paddington became ever more inconvenient. By May 1844 the Bristol & Exeter was opened throughout to Exeter, by June 1844 the line was opened to Oxford, by May 1845 to Gloucester, by September 1850 to Banbury. During 1852 the line was completed to Birmingham and South Wales. These extensions caused the Company to consider more permanent arrangements. It was not, however, the lack of facilities within the terminus, which although small had remained fairly adequate, but the lack of an hotel which spurred the Company into action. The Prince of Wales Hotel shown in FIGS 18 and 20 was obviously neither suitable nor good enough for the Company's purposes. Its size in the various illustrations is almost certainly exaggerated, and it was probably nothing more than a Public House with rooms. Also the Company

26. The five remaining arches of the original Bishop's Bridge. The north-eastern arch is partially obscured by a brick pillar built in front of it. There is a sixth arch to the south west, which is completely bricked up. Just beyond this is the steel lattice-girder bridge which replaced the main spans of the Bishop's Bridge in 1907. (The author)

41

27. View looking south. The brick pillar in the foreground is part of the structure of the later goods office, now demolished, which fronted Bishop's Bridge Road. (The author)

95. PRO RAIL 250/4, Board Minutes, 21/11/1850.

96. Ibid.,5/12/1850. (The London and Birmingham and Grand Junction Railways amalgamated in July 1846 to form the London & North Western Railway.)

97. Ibid., 12 & 19/12/1850.

98. Quoted in MacDermot, op. cit.

99. Ibid.

did not own it and hotels were becoming an important part of railway business at this time.

On 4 November 1850 St George Burke KC, the Company's Parliamentary Agent, wrote to the Company stating:

The inconvenience which at present exists in not having an Hotel in the neighbourhood suitable for passengers travelling by the railway . . .

The letter was read and discussed at the board meeting of 21 November[95] and two directors were requested to meet St George Burke to discuss the matter further. At a meeting on 5 December, after discussing possible sites for the hotel, the following resolution was adopted:

That the advantages of securing to Travellers a good London Hotel near the Terminus of a Railway points out the necessity to this Company of promoting it especially when the competition thro. the districts in

Oxfordshire, Warwickshire and the North with the London & North Western Company may decide Passengers to adopt either the one line or the other according to the comparative convenience of an hotel in London.[96]

At further meetings on the 12 and 19 December[97] the matter was again discussed and at the latter meeting:

Mr Brunel afterwards attended the Board and submitted Ground Plans of the intended Passenger Station at Paddington such as he considered to be necessary in order to determine the most eligible position for building the proposed Hotel which must obviously depend upon the permanent arrangements for the Traffic of the line.

Plans for the hotel and permanent terminus were finally approved in February 1851.

Initially the Company wished to build a new passenger departure shed only, beyond the goods shed – the new goods shed to be to the north of the temporary station. By the end of 1852 most of the old goods shed had been removed and work on the new departure side well advanced. Early in 1853 the directors decided to go ahead with the permanent arrival shed. In August 1853 Brunel reported:

The works at Paddington Station for the passenger trains are still much in arrear, but are advancing towards completion. The alteration of the main lines, approaching Paddington, has been effected, and the Engine-house is in course of construction upon the site of the original line of Railway. As soon as it is completed, the old Engine-house may be removed and the extension of the Goods Department, now much needed, may be commenced.[98]

The new station was opened for departure traffic on 16 January and for arrivals on 29 May 1854. A detailed analysis and history of the construction of the new terminus must be the subject for another book. However, the period from 1851 to

1854, and beyond, was one of considerable upheaval which Brunel aptly sums up:

> ... the difficulties of proceeding successively with different portions of the new work on the site of old buildings, without interfering too much with the carrying on of the traffic in a Station, already far too small for the wants, have been very great . . .[99]

These words must sum up the thoughts of many a project manager since that time.

The only visible remains of the original terminus are the five north-eastern arches of the original Bishop's Bridge at grid reference TQ265816 (FIGS 26–29). The larger, south-western arch is possibly the original arrival exit, see FIG.11, and the cloakroom and lost property office would have been immediately to the south of it. The main part of the original Bishop's Bridge was demolished in 1907 and replaced by the present steel lattice-girder structure.

28 (left). Inside of the south-western arch showing bricked-up cross passages. (The author)

29 (above). View looking north west. The wide arch to the left is possibly the original arrival exit. (The author)

Great Western Railway Book of Reference, November 1836

Received in the Office of the Clerk of the Peace for Middlesex, the 30th day of November 1836
– Attached to the Parliamentary Deposited Plan.[100]

For the Parliamentary Deposited Plan refer to FIG.10 which shows plots 12 to 39.

NO. ON PLAN	DESCRIPTION OF PROPERTY	OWNERS OR REPUTED OWNERS	LESSEES OR REPUTED LESSEES	OCCUPIERS
1	Meadow	William Kinnaird Jenkins		George Wise
2	ditto	ditto		ditto
3	ditto	Richard Aldridge Busby		H. Jackson
4	Occupation Road	ditto, William Gibbs & W.K. Jenkins		
5	Meadow	R.A. Busby		H. Jackson
6	ditto	William Gibbs		John Cockerell
7	ditto	R.A. Busby		H. Jackson
8	ditto	Bishop of London & Trustees of the Paddington Estate		John Cockerell
9	ditto	Richard A. Busby		John Tomlin
10	ditto	Bishop of London & Trustees of the Paddington Estate		Lord Hill
11	ditto	R.A. Busby	John Cockerell	ditto
12	Garden	ditto	ditto	ditto
13	Foot Path	Surveyor of Highways		
14	House outbuildings ground and paddock	John Cockerell		Lord Hill
15	Meadow, Brook and Occupation Road	John Cockerell		Lord Hill
15a	Paddock	Parishioners	John Cockerell	ditto
16	Turnpike Road	Commissioners of the Metropolis Roads North of the Thames		
17	Parish Road	Surveyor of Highways		
18	Meadow	Bishop of London & Trustees of the Paddington Estate		James Darke
19	House outbuildings paddock and grounds	John Cockerell		In hand
20	Meadow	Bishop of London & Trustees of the Paddington Estate		William Palmer
21	Public House Stables Sheds and Garden	John Scales		Edward Minton
22	Garden and Sheds	Bishop of London & Trustees of the Paddington Estate		ditto
23	Cottage	John Scales	Edward Minton	John Hall
24	ditto	ditto	ditto	Messrs Taylor and Messrs Myers
25	Sheds and Yards	ditto		Edward Minton
26	Brook	ditto and Bishop of London & Trustees of the Paddington Estate		
27	Cottage and Garden	Bishop of London & Trustees of the Paddington Estate	E. Keene	Element Keen & J. Morris

100. London Metropolitan Archives.

28	ditto	ditto	Richard Middleton	Richard Middleton & Thomas Hobson
29	Westbourne Street	ditto		
30	Cottage and Gardens	ditto		H. Miles
31	Meadow	ditto		George Stapleton
32	Brick Ground	ditto		ditto
33	Open Ground	Grand Junction Canal Company		In hand
34	Foot path	Surveyor of Highways		
35	Private road	Bishop of London & Trustees of the Paddington Estate		
36	Wharf and Stabling	Grand Junction Canal Company		In hand
37	House Timber Yard and Wharf	ditto	Thomas France	Thomas France
38	Wooden foot bridge and road	ditto or Surveyor of Highways		
39	Open ground	Grand Junction Canal Company		In hand and James Darke

15a is the Bread and Cheese Lands, 34 is the Bishop's Walk

APPENDIX B

Analysis of Construction Costs

Extracted from London General Ledger and London General Journal 1836–1845[101]

April–December 1837

PADDINGTON TERMINUS

Wages		£36,870
Brickwork Grissell & Peto	18,887	
B.&N. Sherwood	11,143	30,030
Iron and Ironwork		2,699
Timber		5,693
Rails, Sleepers and Chairs		3,813
Wheels, Waggons and Barrows Etc.		3,592
Stone and Gravel		1,195
Glazing		64
Miscellaneous and unidentified items		1,504

Total for April–December 1837   £85,460

January 1838–December 1839

PADDINGTON TERMINUS

Wages		£33,903
Brickwork Grissell & Peto	20,101	
B.&N. Sherwood	16,280	36,381
Iron and Ironwork		3,973
Timber		2,358
Glass and Glazing		351
Gravel, Ballast and Forming roads		2,774
Miscellaneous and unidentified items		8,354

PADDINGTON STATION
General construction costs including: fitting out, ironwork, lamp posts, laying pipes and machinery   5,439

PADDINGTON ENGINE HOUSE
General construction costs

B.&N. Sherwood	1,402
Other items	216

PADDINGTON MERCHANDISE STATION
Brickwork and general construction costs

Grissell & Peto	1,799	
B.&N. Sherwood	700	
Thos. Cooper	366	
J.&C. Rigby	2,000	4,865
Turntables		285
Cranes		267
Miscellaneous and unidentified items		184

PADDINGTON STABLES
Brickwork and general construction costs

B.&N. Sherwood	846

Total for January 1838–December 1839   £101,598

January 1840–December 1841

PADDINGTON TERMINUS

Wages		2,103
Brickwork and general construction costs		
Cooper & Scarlett	465	
B.&N. Sherwood	4,081	
Grissell & Peto	231	
Thos. Cooper	1,088	5,865
Gravel and forming roads		
Wm Nicholls		4,566

101. PRO RAIL 272/38–42, London General Ledger, and RAIL 272/67–71, London General Journal, 1836–1845.

Ironwork		1,255
Miscellaneous and unidentified items		950

PADDINGTON STATION
Brickwork and general construction costs

B.&N. Sherwood	2,786	
Cooper & Scarlett	116	
Thos. Cooper	839	
J.&C. Rigby	1,350	5,091
Gravel and roads		283
Miscellaneous and unidentified items		879

PADDINGTON CARRIAGE STATION
General construction costs

J.&C. Rigby	1,427	
Thos. Cooper	499	
J.A. Abbott	2,573	
J.&C. Rigby & Thos. Cooper	3,147	7,646
Ironwork		272
Miscellaneous and unidentified items		625

PADDINGTON MERCHANDISE STATION
General construction costs

J.&C. Rigby & Thos. Cooper	883
Cranes	45
Gravel	219
Miscellaneous and unidentified items	140

Total for January 1840–December 1841   **£30,822**

January 1842–December 1843

PADDINGTON TERMINUS

Brickwork and general construction costs	621
Ironwork	26
Roads etc.	323
Miscellaneous and unidentified items	241

PADDINGTON STATION
Brickwork and general construction costs

J.&C. Rigby and Thos. Cooper	411	
J.A. Abbott	135	546
Cranes		166
Ironwork		502
Miscellaneous and unidentified items		155

Total for January 1842–December 1843   **£2,580**

January 1844–December 1845

PADDINGTON TERMINUS

Roads Etc.	493

PADDINGTON STATION

Miscellaneous and unidentified items	120

PADDINGTON CARRIAGE STATION
General construction costs

J. Heard	1,025	
Thos. Cooper	753	1,778
Traversing Frames		145
Miscellaneous and unidentified items		1,811

PADDINGTON MERCHANDISE STATION
Brickwork and general construction costs

J.&C. Rigby and Thos. Cooper	2,101
John Porter, Iron Roofing	450
Crane	147
Miscellaneous and unidentified items	187

PADDINGTON ENGINE HOUSE

Miscellaneous and unidentified items	170

PADDINGTON NEW OFFICES (OVER CARRIAGE STATION)
Brickwork and general construction costs

J.A. Abbott	3,011
Miscellaneous and unidentified items	746

Total for January 1844–December 1845   **£11,159**

Summary 1837–1845

Brickwork and general construction costs

Grissell & Peto	41,018	
B.&N. Sherwood	37,238	
Cooper & Scarlett	581	
Thos. Cooper	3,545	
J.&C. Rigby	4,777	
Thos. Cooper and J.&C. Rigby	7,163	
J.A. Abbott	5,735	
J. Heard	1,025	
General – unspecified	5,809	106,891
Iron and ironwork		9,177
Timber		8,051
Rails, sleepers, chairs, waggons and barrows		7,405
Cranes, turntables, traversing frames etc.		1,055
Glass and glazing		415
Stone, gravel ballast etc., and forming roads		9,853
Other – miscellaneous and unidentified items		15,896
Wages (1837–1841)		72,876

Total for 1837–1845   **£231,619**

Estimates

(1) From Brunel's private letterbook 2, October 1836 to April 1837[102] (in a clerk's hand)

Great Western Railway Extension

Estimate

Earthwork	200,000 @ 1/6	
	350,000 @ 1/-	32,500
Masonry		11,000
Forming Permanent Road*		24,850
		68,350
10 Per Cent		6,835
		75,185
Land		170,000
Total		**£245,185**

*Permanent Way

(2) Read at the Half-Yearly General Meeting of Shareholders, 15 August 1838[103]

Estimates (based on the actual cost of that portion which has been completed)

London division

London to Maidenhead (Extension Act 1837)

Paddington to Acton. Distance 4½ miles.

Land and compensation, including 39 acres for Paddington Depot and 156 acres beyond it.	£175,000
Earthwork, 580,000 cube yards including formation of the embankment at Spring Street, Bishop's Road, Westbourne Road, Ranelagh and Porchester Streets, Black Lion Turnpike Road and subordinate embankments, 2,450 yards run. Metropolitan Turnpike Road embankment, 750 yards run, and gravel and granite for roads.	56,444
Brickwork in mortar and cement including also culverts and main sewer 1,311 yards run, small drains 2,387 yards run, masonry 125,000 cubic feet.	62,508
Passenger sheds, coach house, engine house and fitter's shop, viaduct fittings, construction of shops, sheds and fittings, turntables and traversing frames, sheerlegs, tackle, tarpauling, drain tiles and iron cess pools, fencing etc.	27,328
Sundries.	4,400
Paddington Extension Works.	83,366
Permanent way, including rails, timber screws, felt, bolts and other materials,with labour in laying packing, repacking, keyanising and every other expense incidental thereto at the rate of £9,173 per mile.	41,178
Total	**£450,224**

102. University of Bristol, op. cit.

103. PRO RAIL 250/64, 6th Half Yearly General Meeting, 15/8/1838.

INDEX